Endorsements

As you read SallyAnne's book, you can feel her pain and frustration through the many challenges she faced during her early years. Her writing style is as if she is sitting across from me sharing her story over a cup of coffee. As God set her free of all the stuff, SallyAnne encourages others through her compassion to become the person that God created them to be. Her story will no doubt inspire, encourage, enlighten, and transform all who read it.

—Pat Fehlman, President of the
Redbud Group, LLC, North Canton, Ohio

Stop Dragging Your Stuff Around and allow SallyAnne's life experiences and encounter with Jesus to encourage you and show you how to let go and be free.

—Kim Miller, Arise from the
Ashes Ministries, Copley, Ohio

Still Dragging Your Stuff Around?

Still Dragging Your Stuff Around?

Transforming Your Life

SALLYANNE TRISSEL

TATE PUBLISHING
AND ENTERPRISES, LLC

Published by Tate Publishing & Enterprises, LLC
127 E. Trade Center Terrace | Mustang, Oklahoma 73064 USA
1.888.361.9473 | www.tatepublishing.com

Tate Publishing is committed to excellence in the publishing industry. The company reflects the philosophy established by the founders, based on Psalm 68:11,
"The Lord gave the word and great was the company of those who published it."

Book design copyright © 2013 by Tate Publishing, LLC. All rights reserved.
Cover design by Rtor Maghuyop
Interior design by Mary Jean Archival

Published in the United States of America

ISBN: 978-1-62746-188-7
1. Religion / General
2. Religion / Christian Life / Personal Growth
13.06.06

Dedication

I dedicate this book to the love of my life,
Bill Trissel, otherwise known as my Prince William,
For all of your support and encouragement
And especially for loving me for who I am.

Acknowledgments

I want to thank my friend Nancy Shankle for all her prayers of encouragement to make this book a reality.

A special thank-you to my wonderful therapist, Amy Frankel, for all her support and dedication to show me how to release all that painful stuff I kept dragging around.

I give my heartfelt thanks to Pastor Marykay Moore and all my soul sisters for encouraging me to write during our monthly writing groups and writing retreats.

Thanks to Tate Publishing for believing in me and making this dream come true. And most of all, I am giving the glory to God for allowing his words to flow through me and onto the pages of this book.

Contents

Introduction

Are you tired of all this stuff inside you, around you, behind you, stuff that drains all your energy? I am talking about past issues, anger, resentment, bitterness, pain, just to name a few. Yes, I can relate. I have dragged this stuff around for most of my life. This book is about the years and years that I allowed this messy pain to drag on and on. I tried for many times to dump it, but it seemed to follow me wherever I went. What was worse, it seemed to attract more stuff. I found myself crawling and desperately looking for ways to get away from it. I tried ignoring the stuff since it was behind me, and if I didn't look back, I didn't see it, but sooner or later, it would bounce back, reminding me that it was still there.

I grew up knowing some about God, Jesus, and the nativity but not much more. When I was little, we prayed the simple prayer "God is great. God is good, let us thank him for our food" before we ate supper. Other than that I never saw my parents pray. At church, we sang hymns and listened to the sermon, but it seemed more of a social gathering. So I didn't know about God like I do now.

We all go through different seasons in our life, times when there are valleys and peaks. I was taught to work hard and be kind to others and, mostly, to do the best I could to survive. Yes, I swam upstream quite a bit till I realized that life was much easier to go with the flow of God.

This book tells of all the stuff, pain, and anger, which I held onto most of my life. My hope is to encourage you and let you know that God can do everything and he still performs amazing miracles today. He is a wonderful God who loves us. He created each and every one of us. He planned our journey before we were born. He brought healing into my life and showed me how to release this stuff, to forever bury it and find peace. He can do the same for you.

These past years I found what true peace is. Before, it was just a pretty sounding word, but I never felt peace, to really know peace and to feel the calm of knowing all is well.

In these pages you will read about the bondage I lived under and how I was finally set free to be myself. I was always told I wasn't good enough, so I grew up feeling like I had no value. Today I feel so good and there is so much joy in my life. My attitude has changed and I don't sweat the small stuff anymore. And, my new friend, my reader, you can find this peace too! Read along with me and you will learn about the depression and the life I overcame.

This is the story how God transformed me from the frumpy caterpillar who kept dragging all her painful stuff behind her, to being healed to find the freedom

to fly free. God showed me how to forgive myself and helped me to forgive others who had hurt me. You will see how God helped me to release the dark pain from the deepest crevices of my soul to bring it to the surface where God's light could shine upon it, healing it once and for all. I found the peace from the pain that held me hostage for many years. My prayer is that you will find hope and God will give you grace and mercy to follow your purpose in life.

Born Free

> So that you may live a life worthy of the Lord and please him in every way: bearing fruit in every good work, growing in the knowledge of God.
>
> Colossians 1: 10

Let me start by explaining how I came to be. My mom had a very rough life. She became ill with polio when she was only eight years old. I was told that her leg became so crippled that the doctor wanted to amputate it. My grandma was against the amputation and refused to have my mom's leg removed. I am happy to report that I never saw any weakness in my mom's leg; evidently, she was a miracle and totally recovered.

Mom had been married before she met my dad. I am telling you this to help you understand more about my mom, which I will later share in the book. I only heard a few things about her first husband. He was a truck driver and they had married when she was only sixteen. I could see her eyes sparkle when she spoke of him. I could tell she had loved him very much. They were married around 1936. Folks were having rough times finding food for their families, but Mom and her husband did all right.

They never had any children, and during their tenth year of marriage, he died of spinal meningitis. When there was a contagious illness, they quarantined the homes back then and the doctors made house calls. In the event of a quarantined home, family members were locked in. No one could enter the home or leave. Mom became a widow at twenty-six.

I never heard how Mom actually met my Dad, but I knew he was in the army and stationed in Okinawa, Japan. They married a year after her first husband died. My mom always wanted children, so my parents tried unsuccessfully for quite a while before her doctor found a problem with her fallopian tubes. She had an operation to repair the damage. This is probably why she never had children with her first husband.

After she recovered, they conceived and my brother was born later that year. Unfortunately this was a breech birth. In other words, he was born feet first. Once again, this was long before the medical technology of today. This birth was a long and struggling labor for my mom. I heard it was fifty-two hours of labor. She delivered a healthy blond baby boy and they named him Joseph John Kornish and nicknamed him Joey.

After another year and a half, Mom delivered a stillborn baby boy. They named him Mark. Burying this little baby broke my mom's heart; she became very depressed. My brother, Joey, was the light in her world then. I believe he, along with God, gave her the strength to pull herself back together.

When Joey was three years old, my mom was determined to try for another child. Her doctors were

against the idea as well as my dad. I believe in my heart that this may be why my dad was never close to his children—just a feeling I have. Having another baby was such a risk to her health let alone the recent emotional pain of the loss of her last baby. Everyone told her she should be thankful for her little boy and forget about another baby. Since I am writing this, I am sure you have figured out by now that she was successful and blessed with a baby girl. They named me Sally Anne Kornish. I weighed six pounds and was twenty-two inches long and had coal black hair, which stuck straight up. I have heard that my father looked at me and had said that someday she will be pretty. So I named this chapter "Born Free," since I was like everyone else, born free and innocent. Babies are such miracles. They come into this world with nothing and are dependent on their parents to survive. So I was born free, pure, and was a very long, skinny, and not so pretty baby girl.

When I was about three, I was out in the backyard sitting in a blow-up–type swimming pool. I had my swimming suit on and was playing in the water. Without going into all the details, my uncle forever changed my life that day. He was outside walking around the yard when he approached me in my pool. This man molested me, and at that moment, I lost that precious little girl. My innocent, young mind buried this painful memory deep inside. That day I placed the first few bricks to begin building that huge wall to hide behind and protect my inner child. I became so withdrawn and so shy. I was too young to understand, and I never told anyone.

I later learned that my inner child became lost and had hidden deep inside because of all the pain. It wasn't till I was in my thirties that this all boiled up to the surface and showed its ugly head. I became so angry and depressed. I found a therapist who tried her best to relieve my depression and advised me to go for hypnosis to search for a cause of my anger. Have you ever had hypnosis? No, it isn't like the entertainers who make you walk like a chicken. They actually take you in a quiet room and put you in a state of calmness. I can remember the doctor had me picture myself on a train, but this train went backward. The train departed at the point of where I was currently in my life, and as it went backward, I could see billboards with years on them. Occasionally, I was stopped at certain years and asked what I saw, where I was in that year. It was really cool. They took me way, way back to where there were no billboards. What is this? They asked me what I saw. I saw darkness and it felt really tight there. Then I could see a beautiful white dove fly off into the light. Then I felt alive and free. Amazingly, I was told that this was my birth. Can you imagine? Wow. I just lived through my birth. Then he brought me forward for a while and stopped. What do you see now? I was asked. It was so real. I could actually see life as I saw it from my view as a little girl. I was standing in my playpen giggling as I could see my brother smiling at me through the rungs. I could see the entire room as it was back then. I had to be only a year old. I really wanted to stay there but I was put back on the train. I was sent forward, and all of a sudden, I started crying, actually sobbing so hard. I

could see my uncle's face and I started screaming. It was so painful, so scary. I was there. I couldn't stop sobbing. The doctor told me that they didn't need to put me through any more pain. They had found the reason why I was suffering.

After the session they allowed me to sit quietly and listen to some relaxing music. It didn't relax me though. I left the office in a state of confusion. I felt lost as if I was in outer space and had landed here on earth. It took several days to finally get back into my world as it was.

I couldn't hold any anger toward this evil man. I never liked him, and thankfully he never touched me again. You see, he had died many years before. But before he passed, my aunt, who was my mom's sister, had suffered a cerebral hemorrhage at the age of forty-five. After she passed, my uncle hooked up a trailer to the back of his car. He kept all her material possessions in this trailer and her urn of ashes beside him in the front seat. He traveled with that trailer for many years. He was a very sick man. When he had died, they found his naked body under a kitchen table. He had shot himself in the head. He had two brothers, and they also had killed themselves, one by hanging and the other shot himself. All three brothers committed suicide.

Childhood Stuff

Love the Lord your God with all your heart and
with all your soul and with all your strength and
with all your mind.

Luke 10: 27

I was raised a country girl long before they had cell
phones. My family was not outgoing and my parents
never visited much. My dad worked a lot. He always
worked hard. He was a boiler man engineer for a steel
factory. I never saw my dad watch a sporting event on
television let alone go to a game. The only TV shows I
remember him watching were the old shows *Bonanza*,
Rifleman, *Gunsmoke* to name a few. He didn't have any
hobbies; he just worked.

Mom was a stay-at-home mom and was always
doing embroidery in her spare time. My dad was a very
controlling man and Mom had to live her life the way
he demanded. She had to have meals on the table along
with a homemade dessert when he expected them. She
always had to be home when and if he called from
work. She didn't have any close friends and lived a very
lonely life. My dad was a jealous man and didn't want

her to have friends or work outside of home. But Dad worked very hard and worked many different shifts. I always expected when he worked the midnight shift that he would become very mean and abusive. He would literally explode in anger. Since my brother was older, he was never at home. He was out doing guy stuff or he was picking fruit for a job at the orchard down the street. He never seemed to be around much. I was the little girl who wrapped herself around her mommy's apron. I never went anywhere.

There were some camping trips when we would stay at a lake for the weekend. I loved to fish and had my bamboo pole and loved sitting by the water. I could sit there for hours waiting for my red-and-white bobber to bounce up and down. If I was lucky enough to catch a fish, it was usually a small blue gill or catfish. After removing the hook, I always threw the fish back into the lake.

These were some good memories sleeping in the musty old tent crowded together in our sleeping bags. We didn't do much as a family so I cherished those camping trips. We would build a fire and cook our food outdoors. I loved to roast marshmallows in the evening.

My cousins lived far away and I was the youngest. I didn't see my relatives much while growing up. Our family stayed at home. My dad's parents came from Poland and Grandpa had died before I was born. Grandma didn't speak English and I can't even remember her ever calling me by my name. I remember Mom's parents a little more even though they died young. Grandpa died of Leukemia when I was five. I have fond memories

of my grandma and I coloring in a coloring book. She might have been the one who ignited my passion for artwork. I don't know. She died when I was about eight. I never had close relatives and even close friends. I was very shy and hid behind my mom if someone like a neighbor came around.

After I finished kindergarten, we moved to Zoar, Ohio. Zoar was a small historical town where the Germans came and settled down. We owned the grocery store and I really had fun there. This building had many floors and we lived upstairs. It was hard for my parents to run the store since this was a very quaint town and people did not have much money. I went to first grade, and the following summer, we sold the store and moved closer to Canton. My parents lived in this house for the rest of their lives.

I started second grade and was thrilled to make friends with the neighborhood children. We spent many a night playing board games or hide-and-seek. We had good times and a lot of memories were made in those backyards. After those days life seemed to go fast, and soon I was in high school. My brother graduated and was attending the technical school in our town.

This is the time of my life when I developed my artistic skills. I love to paint and my brother always encouraged me. Joey was always the one to buy my art supplies for my birthday or special occasions.

Mom was always sick. She was a smoker and her bronchial asthma always had her coughing. Her smoking disgusted me. I know she smoked because of her nerves and he never seemed to be happy. He just worked all the

time. If he wasn't working during the summer, he was busy mowing our large lawn.

Mom was always very depressed and lying down a lot. When Dad would get mean to her, I would step in between them to guard her, which meant I always got the belt. I can remember Dad in such a rage where he picked me up by my ankles and banged my head into the floor, several fillings fell out of my teeth. I am sure since I protected my mom, he became more distant with me. I never really knew my dad and I grew to hate him so much.

When I was a sophomore in high school, I was very involved in art classes. There was this senior girl who was so gifted and talented. Peg was so popular and was friends with everyone. I would look at her paintings while wishing my artwork was as good as hers. I can remember her self portrait, which was done in oils. The painting was magnificent and looked just like her. She, along with several other art class students, had gone to Europe the previous summer on an art study course. I would hear her talk often about all the different countries they visited and how much fun it was. Oh, how I envied her. I was so shy and stayed to myself, wishing I had friends, but I never seemed to fit in.

The next year they announced that they were going to take another trip to study abroad during the summer. I was so excited. I kept asking my parents if I could go. I secretly felt that if I could go, I would come back popular like Peg did. I bugged my parents day in and day out. I wanted to go to Europe. At the time was brother had enlisted into the air force. Since he was my encourager, he helped me talk my parents into letting me go.

The Red Suitcase

Oh my bed I remember you; I think of you
through the watches of the night. Because you
are my help, I sing in the shadow of your wings.
I cling to you, your right hand upholds me.

Psalm 63: 6–8

My junior year had ended and it was time to start
packing for my trip to Europe. Since I would
be starting my senior year that fall, I had to have my
senior pictures taken. There wouldn't be time after the
trip for we would be overseas for six weeks. What was I
going to wear? I knew I would wear the air force wing
necklace that my brother had given me. I decided on a
soft yellow sweater. The photographer shoot went well
and the pictures would be ready before school started.

I needed to find a good durable suitcase. I found a
bright red one and I knew it would be perfect. The study
tour group sent the itinerary of where and when I would
be in different locations. They sent along a suggested list
of items I would need. We got the passport, traveler's
checks, and I had gotten the preventative shots from the
doctor. I was all packed and ready to leave. But now I am

scared to death. The reality that I was really going had set in and I did not want to leave home. I had never flown before, let alone fly to another country. As Mom and I pulled into the airport, I was panic stricken and crying. We went inside and met the others. There were six of us going from my art club including my art teacher. When it was time to board our flight, my mom literally had to push me toward the plane. This was 1969, and security was much different. Family and friends could walk out with you as you boarded. I tearfully hugged Mom good-bye and reluctantly climbed the steps and found my seat.

After we had settled into our seats, I was still crying and very scared. I was a homebody, never left my mom's side other than to go to school. This kind lady seated next to me was reassuring me that everything was going to be okay as the plane whisked down the runway. Soon we were heading up through the clouds. Finally I started feeling calmer knowing I made it this far. We were on our way. It didn't seem long till we were ready to land in New Jersey. Whew, by the time we were on the ground again, I actually began to like to fly.

We had to commute to the New York airport by taxi. This was where the international flights departed. We stopped along the way at a restaurant for supper. We had a few hours before we were scheduled to be at the airport. I started feeling comfortable and enjoyed being away from home. Reality was settling in. I was going to be spending the summer in Europe.

As we began boarding this huge airplane, I was nervous but also very excited. This was a six-hour overnight flight. The stewardess was busy passing out

blankets and pillows as we tried to get comfortable in our seats. The engines started and soon we were off on our way, climbing straight up into the sky. Everyone around me seemed to be going to sleep, but I had my eyes wide open with enthusiasm. I don't think I closed them at all during the flight. My thoughts of anticipation of all the excitement and all the places we would visit was overwhelming me. Soon the stewardess was preparing us for landing and the plane became alive with chatter. We were all sitting up in our seats and were about to land in Rome, Italy. The plane skidded on the runway, and soon it came to a stop. We are here.

After we unloaded and gathered our luggage, we tried to locate the rest of the group on our tour. There were 111 of us from all over the United States. That was some undertaking locating everyone. There were lots of college kids in this group and they were now in a foreign country. I could tell that they were very excited to be away from home and planning on lots of partying. Oh boy. This plain old country girl felt very alone although I was ready to enjoy this trip.

We were all scheduled to stay in dormitories and some Catholic schools. We all boarded three huge tour buses, which took us to our first stop, a large brick building. This was a place where nuns studied. We carried our suitcases up many flights of stairs till we were directed to our rooms. My room was small with a twin bed and it had a bathroom. We could unpack since we would be staying here for a week. We were told about our study schedule, to arise early for breakfast so we could be in the classroom by nine the next morning. We were going

to be studying about the famous artists as well as the fine architecture of the early cathedrals.

Since I did not sleep much on the flight over, I was tired but so excited to be in Rome. I went to my room to be by myself even though I heard the others gathering in a room down the hall. I didn't feel comfortable since I am so shy, so I lay down on my bed to enjoy the quiet and fell asleep.

The alarm clock rang as I rubbed my eyes trying to gather my senses. Yes, I am in Rome. I dressed and headed to the dining room and was happy to find a seat next to one of my friends from school. Breakfast looked interesting—oatmeal, orange juice, hot tea, and a hard roll. I was very hungry so I ate it all and gathered my books and headed to the classroom.

Our instructor was up front talking to some kids as I found a seat. Some of the other girls from school were sitting close by. The instructor was a handsome Italian guy who spoke broken English. He told us that we would meet Monday through Friday down in this classroom from nine in the morning till noon. We would be excused for lunch and then go out in groups to visit the different locations for our homework

Over the next week we saw the Coliseum, Spanish Steps, the Vatican, the Sistine Chapel, and St. Peter's Basilica. There was so much going on. My head was spinning with excitement. We were instructed not to drink the water or eat any uncooked fruits or vegetables because of the way they fertilize their gardens. It was interesting seeing how different the Italians lived.

We moved to a Mexican university. Yes, I did say Mexican. We were now on the outskirts of Rome in the country. This was a newer building with a locked, gated security entrance. There was a long lane/driveway connecting you to the main road. We all got settled in to our new rooms. After supper we went to the large lounge to study.

The next morning during class I started feeling sick. After telling the instructor I was ill, I left and went quickly to my room. They called in a doctor as well as an interpreter. I was so sick in bed when they arrived. When the doctor started examining me, he tapped on my stomach. We were always told to wear our money belts under our clothes, so as he tapped, you could hear the tingling of the change. His eyes opened so wide and the look on his face was so funny. I reached under my shirt to expose the pink satin money belt. The interpreter and doctor started to laugh along with me. Unfortunately it was determined that I had dysentery. I was given a prescription for diarrhea and stomach cramps. No food other than dry toast and hot tea for the next few days. These pills actually looked like horse pills—they were huge. I also had to drink this vial of liquid medicine, yucky. I had to stay in bed for a few days while the rest of the group went out of town on an excursion. The staff at this facility came in to check on me and bring my tea and toast. Talk about lonely. No one spoke English and I was sick and scared. So the next few days I cried and slept a lot. Finally the others were back and I was so happy to see them. I was feeling much better and the doctor released me to continue with the study tour.

A few of my friends felt so bad for me that they wanted to take me out for supper. The building where we were staying had the entrance down a long lane. As we walked to the end of the lane, we got a taxi, which would take us into town. We decided to get a pizza. This was nothing like any pizza I have ever seen before. It had a baked dough crust with an oily tomato sauce, nothing else, no pepperoni or vegetables. It was definitely different but it tasted so good, especially since I hadn't had any real food for days. It was just so great being out of my room and laughing with the girls. It started to get dark so we got a taxi to head back to our building.

Walking down this long lane we could see a bunch of Italian guys waiting by the gate. I am sure the word got out that American girls were staying there. We were told later that American girls have a reputation of being fast since Italian girls stayed home cooking and doing chores. As we nervously approached the locked gate, one of the girls ran to push the intercom button. No one answered. These guys started surrounding us and laughing in their native tongue.

"Please! Please, open the gate! Help us!" the girl screamed out while pushing the intercom. Still, no one responded.

All of a sudden, I could feel the breath of the tallest one breathing on my neck. Next he started to kiss me, and I tried desperately to push him away. He grabbed me and pushed me to the ground. He then climbed on top of me and started touching me. I could hear my blouse being torn.

"Please! Please! Open the gate," she screamed.

I could hear the others yelling and screaming as they were also being attacked. Then all of a sudden the guys started yelling. The girl at the intercom had sprayed her mace toward these guys.

She had sprayed the guy on me also. As he started yelling, he rubbed his eyes, and I squirmed away from under him. We all scrambled away as the gate finally opened. We were pulling each other by the arms, and we ran through the entrance, never looking back. Still shaking, we ran into the dormitories yelling for help. We reported to the authorities of this school what had happened. We were all so devastated with fear, this was more than I could handle. I went to my room to hide under the covers. I could not stop crying, and I wanted to go home.

The next night it happened again to a couple other girls on this tour. But this time they were raped and badly beaten. It could have been us.

After that experience I was happy to know we were leaving the next morning for Venice. After we awoke and had breakfast, we were packed and loaded on those tour buses and on our way. I felt safe to finally rest as we traveled through this beautiful land. After a few hours, the buses arrived on the outskirts of Venice. We pulled up to this old dark brick building. Actually all the buildings were old. They had so much character as well as history. I loved checking out the old structures. Some of these quaint places had painted artwork on the ceilings. Another thing I should mention, we never got used to carrying our suitcases up the multiple staircases. These places had to have lodging for all of us, 111 of us.

Most of the time, the buses had to park quite a distance away from where we were staying. Trust me! We tried to keep our luggage as light as possible. Every night I washed my clothes by hand and hung them in the bathroom to dry.

After lunch we rode the water taxis over to Venice. We got out of the boat and we went on our separate ways in smaller groups to see some sights. I wanted to ride in a gondola; after all, we were in Venice. I was excited to see that they wore red-and-white striped shirts as they steered the boats with these long paddles through the canals of the city. You could see up close how they lived and their homes. And yes, the gondolier sang as we went along on our trip. We got off and went looking for more places to see. They had lots of outside markets selling all sorts of stuff. I found a cute dress and my friend found a purse. The weather was warm and sunny and we were having fun.

We continued on through the town excitedly checking everything out. We could hear music in the distance. The rest of the girls from our group joined us. We were curious to see where the music was coming from. As we got closer we saw people dancing and singing. There were musicians playing guitars along with other instruments. We watched for quite a while until we realized that it was getting late. We went to find the water taxis to get back across the water. We found out the taxis stopped running in the evening. And once again here we were stuck with all these drunken Italian guys with no way back to our building. I was so scared. Please, Lord, help us girls find a way back. What were

we going to do? We bravely tried to keep calm while walking around looking for a possible way to get across the water to our building.

It started to get darker, and the place began to swarm with Italian men. All I wanted to do was run and hide. I was shaking and scared to death. These men would walk up to us and brush against us, trying to get as close as possible. I just kept walking away from them. The music became louder, and it was so crowded that it was hard to walk between these people.

We could see these small boats docked along side. One of the girls said she had an idea. She approached this young man standing next to a boat. She started talking to him, but he spoke little English. She asked if this was his boat and smiling, he nodded yes to my beautiful blonde friend. She next asked him if he could take her friends across the water. He seemed more than happy to. I believe he wanted to see her after we were dropped off.

He actually seemed very nice since he offered his hand to help us get on board. It was very dark except for the light reflecting from the street light on the water as we left the dock. We were still very scared and hoping her plan would get us back safe. As we got closer to land, we could see the street light shining on our building. As the boat bumped into the dock, we quickly climbed out and all of us, even my blonde friend waved good-bye as we ran to our lodging. The sad, lonely Italian guy was left standing in his boat. I know we were stupid and could have gotten hurt. Who knows what this guy could have had in mind. Praise the Lord, we were soon safe

in our rooms. This was another night that I went to bed wishing I was home, snuggled under my own cozy quilt.

Over the next few weeks, we visited Paris and some other small French towns. I was not impressed with Paris. It was dirty. We went to the Louvre where the painting of Mona Lisa is. Did you know that the painting is real small? Maybe eighteen inches by twenty-four inches. The Louvre has beautiful gardens. We also saw the Versailles Castle with all of its gorgeous landscaping and floral gardens. And, of course, you have to go up in the Eiffel tower while in Paris. We visited Notre Dame Cathedral and enjoyed how fabulous this structure is, so historic. We continued with our studies, enjoying all the sights we could as well as taking good notes of all the places we visited. We were reminded that we would have exams at the end of our trip.

During the end of our fifth week, we went to Luzern, Switzerland. The scenery traveling there was fabulous. Most of the roads were small, curving up the mountains in those huge buses. But amazingly we always made it there. The buses couldn't park close to our lodging and we had to carry our luggage up a steep hill till we came to the building. This was an old convent. We stayed here several days seeing all the sights and then we were on our way to Geneva. We were along the Mediterranean Sea and the water was pure blue. Everything about Switzerland was gorgeous—the white snow-capped mountains, the flowing hills and the water, just breathtaking. While we were sightseeing, I had to buy a watch. I was sad to leave this scenic country but we were soon heading back to

France to make our way up to the English Chanel to cross over to England.

As they loaded the buses onto this large ferry, some of us decided to stay outside where we could enjoy the fresh sea air. The seagulls were flying over our heads. The sky was a magnificent shade of blue, not a cloud anywhere. The sun was brightly shining, and we were just enjoying this gorgeous view as the ferry left the dock. As we got closer, we could see the white cliffs of Dover. We departed the ferry and were excited to be heading toward London. These were our last three days of this study tour and we were all tired. The buses pulled up to the next dormitory. We quickly unpacked and prepared to visit the town. They gave us maps and told us which places we were to visit. We were anxious to get busy on our assignments. We boarded a red double-decker bus and headed to the Westminster Abbey Cathedral. We drove past the huge clock tower of Big Ben and crossed the London Bridge. At the Westminster Abbey, I was in awe of the magnificent sculptures and all the history this cathedral had to tell.

The next day we visited Buckingham Palace and saw the Changing of the Guard. Their uniforms were so immaculate and colorful. We tried to get the guards to smile, but they kept their sober expressions no matter what faces we made. Being silly girls we tried so hard to get them to laugh, but they never did.

We visited the national museum and prepared for our last class. Each city we visited had a different instructor to teach our class. Some of the teachers were really nice and kept our attention, but there were a few that were

boring. I often had trouble understanding their accents, but all in all, we had learned so much. It was an awesome opportunity for me. This was a college course and we had to do most of the work by personally visiting the cathedrals, museums, and architectural buildings and bridges. We had paperwork and research notes to be completed. It was really important to listen to the tour guides and take good notes.

It was time to take our last exam and I was anxious to get this over with and go home. The test took an hour and a half. It was quite difficult and I had to struggle to remember some answers. When we were finished, we were told that they would pass out the test results before dinner. We were to pack and prepare to leave after dinner. I was handed my folder and was thrilled that I passed. Whew. Finally the stress was over and I could relax while eating our last meal. But we were also sad for we would soon be saying our good-byes. Since we were from different parts of the United States, we would be taking different flights back. This would be our last time together.

Leaving England, I tearfully boarded the large plane. I was returning home a more mature young lady than the scared little girl who had left home for the first time. I had overcome a lot of horrific experiences, grown, and had become more confident of myself and who I had become. Yes, as a young, naïve, silly American girl who took some risky chances, I had acquired some wisdom. I wasn't as shy and backward as I was when I arrived.

Because of the high price of overseas phone calls, I hadn't called home or talked to my mom for six weeks.

The last time I saw her I was crying as she pushed me up the steps of the plane. I was ready to come home and anxious to unpack this red suitcase. My pretty red suitcase was now adorned with stickers from all the different places it visited along with some dents and scratches from dragging it up and down many flights of stairs.

Just a quick update about the gal named Peg, the one I admired and went on the European study tour to be like her. I found out later that she had become an alcoholic and died at an early age. How sad is that?

Running, No Baggage

God is our refuge and strength, an ever present help in trouble. Therefore we will not fear, though the earth give away and the mountains fall into the heart of the sea.

Psalm 46: 1–2

The flight departed late at night from England. We were all covered with blankets at the stewardess came around and passed out pillows. We tried to get comfortable for the long flight home. I was so exhausted and felt safe up in the sky. These past six weeks were very busy and stressful. My mind was so filled with studying, sightseeing, and just traveling. I must have fallen fast asleep for I was startled when they announced we would soon be landing. I could see the glow of the sun. When you are above the clouds, the sunrise is magnificent. We landed in Newark, New Jersey, and we were thankful to be back on American ground. We had an hour layover before we were to board our final flight to Akron-Canton. It seemed like forever till we boarded our flight and were heading home.

When things got bad during the trip, I always would imagine myself snuggled under my comfy quilt in my own bedroom. I could not wait till I could sleep in my bed again. That was always my sanity during those painful times so far from home.

As the tires skidded on the runway, I anxiously watched out the window looking for my mom. They still allowed visitors to walk out onto the observation deck. Security was nothing like it is today. Anyone could go to the airport and walk out onto the deck just to watch the airplanes take off and land. As our plane taxied closer, I could see my mom waving. It was so good to see her. It seemed like eternity till they let us leave the plane. I quickly ran down the steps to hug my mom. After we got my suitcase, we happily drove home. I was so excited telling her about all the great places I saw when we pulled into the driveway. I was so happy to be home. I went straight inside to my room and jumped on my bed and let out a huge sigh of relief. Exhausted from the long trip, I cuddled up under my comfy quilt and took a nap.

Later after I awoke, some friends called to see if I wanted to go with them to a festival. Oh yes, I would love that, so they came and picked me up. We rode some rides, ate some junk food, and had a great time. I felt like a celebrity as I shared my experiences as a world traveler. After they dropped me off at home, I went inside and Dad was home from work. He was angry and pacing back and forth.

"Where is your mom?" he asked.

I told him that I didn't know. It hurt my feelings since he didn't even welcome me home let alone ask about my trip. But Dad was dad and he would never ask anyway. I became worried and started hoping that Mom wouldn't come home for a while.

"Oh no!" I gasped as I heard the garage door open. I knew she was home. I ran into the kitchen, and Dad followed me. As soon as she opened the door, he started screaming and yelling at her. I have seen this rage before and I was scared for her. He grabbed a hold of her and threw her across the room. She got up and ran toward their bedroom. Before she was able to lock the door, he pushed his way in and locked the door behind him. I could hear her screaming. How can I get her out? I quickly went to the phone and called the sheriff department.

"Help me! My dad is killing my mom!" I screamed into the phone.

"Where is your location?" asked the voice on the phone.

"We live on Fohl Road! Please hurry!"

"There is a squad car on the way. They will be there soon," the voice said.

"Please hurry! I can hear her screams!"

Hanging up the phone, I went and grabbed a baseball bat. I could hear him throwing her around. She began banging on the door, crying out for help. I don't know how, but the door suddenly opened and Mom came running out with Dad grabbing her shoulder. As she ran down the hall, I could see her bloody face and arms. My dad was only wearing his underwear. I ran up and ripped

down his underwear, exposing his privates. Instinctively he let go of Mom to cover himself.

Shaking the bat at him, I screamed at him to stay back.

With Mom protected behind me, I nervously backed us into the kitchen. I could hear a car in the driveway. The deputies had arrived. I took Mom outside with me, and I showed them her bloody, swollen face and nose. Dad had remained inside.

Dad came running outside all dressed and composed and asked, "What happened to her? Was she in a car accident? Why are the deputies here?"

"We are responding to a domestic call, sir."

"Who called you?" asked my dad.

"Sir, we are going to handcuff you and take you into the station!"

"I don't want to press charges," my mom says, crying.

"Then there is nothing we can do other than give this man a warning." You need to go to the hospital. Do you want us to call an ambulance for you?"

My mom shook her head.

"Once again, if you refuse to press charges, there is nothing we can do."

I hated him. He was so arrogant, and what made matters worse, Mom would not press charges against him. I was sick with disgust. After the deputies explained there was nothing they could do since she refused to press charges, they gave Dad a warning and drove away.

It was near midnight and there was no way we were going to stay there. Dad had already taken Mom's car keys. We couldn't drive anywhere. I still had the ball bat, shaking it at Dad, threatening him to stay back. We ran

out the back door and into the connecting wooded area. What else could we do? He was a madman and would kill her and me.

It was dark and very spooky in those woods, but I actually felt more courage out there than stuck in the house with him. I knew these woods connected to a dirt path. It was pitch-black out there and we stumbled on the fallen logs and were getting scratched with prickly bushes. I was happy to find that path that led down behind a neighbor's house. I could see a light on and I was hoping they were still up. I knocked on their back door, and they answered. The neighbor man was alarmed when he saw Mom's bloody face. He motioned for us to come inside. We told him that Dad became explosive and took it out on Mom. He said we could stay for a few days until it was safe to go home. We knew Dad would leave for work in a couple days.

I hadn't even been home a full day and now we were running for our life. Mom told me that Dad had become more possessive and that some coworker was giving him some homemade booze. He had been drinking a lot more.

The neighbors were comforting to us and I was so appreciative for their help. They helped Mom clean her face and we bandaged her nose. It looked like her nose was broken, all swollen and bruised. She had deep scratches and dark bruises everywhere. My mom was a stubborn woman and refused to go to the hospital. Our neighbor man went and got his rifle and kept looking out the window watching for my dad. I really didn't

expect my dad to come looking, and as far as I knew, he didn't.

The neighbors made us some beds with blankets on their couches and we tried to sleep. Once again, all I ever wanted was to be in my own bed. I was grateful for the short nap I had earlier. I was exhausted. Even though I would have rather been home in my own bed, they were very nice and kept us hidden and fed for a few days till Dad left for work.

We called my cousin in town and made arrangements to stay with them. I could see from the road that Dad's truck was gone and he had left for work. We went in the house and gathered some clothes and things we might need for a few weeks. The neighbor was kind enough to drive us into town to my cousin's house. We stayed with my cousin and his family for several months. I shared a room with their two young bratty kids. This was not my choice. But it was what it was.

In the meantime, my school year had started. I drove myself back and forth using my cousin's old car. It ran but not real good. This was not at all the way I planned to start my senior year. If you remember, I was going to be popular. Everyone would want to be my friend and I would be the cool girl like Peg. Wrong! Instead here I was wearing old clothes that really made me feel insecure. I developed a stutter in my speech. I was so withdrawn. I wouldn't even talk to the kids I knew. I just wanted to hide and keep to myself. About my summer trip, forget all that. All this fear and hiding from Dad wiped out those thoughts. I was a real mess.

Eventually Mom contacted a lawyer and we were able to move back into our house. Dad had moved out into a trailer court somewhere. Mom and I did what we could with the little money we could scrape together. Dad was court-ordered to make the house payments and pay the utilities. He never came around and I was thankful. I really hated him. My brother was in the service and we seldom heard from him. There wasn't much money for food or gas, but somehow we always managed to get by. I remained extremely quiet in school and preferred to be left alone. I didn't have many friends and that was okay.

They announced at school that Junior Achievement would start having meetings and they encouraged the students to attend. I thought about it and pushed myself to join. The meetings were held at a hall in town. Large businesses would sponsor smaller companies, giving students a chance to learn about business. We were divided up into small groups that formed into companies. The large businesses would be our mentor and lead us. First we chose our business name and also decided on a product we would make to sell. We would then elect members to become the president, vice president, vice president of sales, secretary, and treasurer. We were students from all the different schools in the county. So I made new friends and gained experience and knowledge about operating a company. I was elected vice president of sales. Whew. That was big for me since I was still very shy and still backward. Hopefully I would become more secure through this experience. We would have meetings with the other company's elected officers.

One evening after a business meeting, this guy who was vice president from another company walked out with me. He seemed like a nice young man. This was back in the days of hippies and Woodstock. Most guys wore their hair long, but this guy had a crew-cut, a clean, well-groomed young man. A few weeks later he asked me out on a date. Looking back now, I should have run as fast as I could. Unfortunately since I was not stable to say the least, this strong, handsome type appealed to me. Jerome was the oldest of four children and showed responsibility. We went out on our first date. Then we went out on a second date, and before long, we were going steady. Couples would exchange class rings, and the girl wore the boy's ring wrapped with fuzzy angora yarn to make it fit her finger. This yarn was so cool and came in all kinds of colors. You would wrap the ring to coordinate with your clothing. If you kept the yarn in the freezer, it would get fluffy. The boy wore the girl's ring on his left pinky.

Let us back up for a moment. Remember that I was living with my mom who was very needy and dependent on all my attention. She was always sick and very demanding. She did not like this young man at all. She did not want me to date and made my life miserable. Even though Mom and I disagreed, Jerome and I continued dating. I was always there for Mom and continued to try my best to make her happy. She was very depressed.

My parents' divorce was final on my graduation day from high school. I drove Mom to the church where the graduation was being held. As I marched with my class

wearing our caps and gowns, I was sad. I was happy to be graduating, but this wasn't what I always pictured it would be like. I don't even know if my dad was there. I never saw him. After I received my diploma, I took Mom home, and I went over to Jerome's graduation party. He had graduated the same night as I did, although we went to different schools. I met his relatives and family friends. They made me feel welcome. He received a complete matching set of luggage for his graduation gift. I didn't receive any graduation gifts.

A few weeks later Jerome moved to Dayton to start technical school. He was taking classes to become a tool and die designer. His school's classes were year-round. While he was gone, I volunteered as a camp counselor for the cerebral palsy. This was the first time that I was around people with physical challenges. I loved it and enjoyed getting to know all about these wonderful folks.

I learned I had compassion and really enjoyed making these kids laugh. I would help them while encouraging them to accomplish their activities. I began to feel like I had value and was seeing a whole new side of who I was.

After the summer camp ended, the director took me aside and told me she felt I had a gift for working with the disabled. She wanted me to go to college and become a speech therapist. What? Me go to college? That was unheard of in my family. Women would stay home and raise their families. Mrs. Wilson was determined to make this happen. I told Mom and she laughed, agreeing that Dad would never help pay for my school. After all, it was already August and school was about to start. I had never given college a second thought. Mrs.

Wilson was persistent. She made arrangements with the university nearby and soon I was enrolled. Amazingly, Dad did help out paying for my first quarter.

I could not believe that within a few weeks I would be a college student. I had to rush and sign up for the classes. Evidently Mrs. Wilson had a big influence there, for everything kept falling into place. I had my books, my class schedules, and even a new sweatshirt with the college logo.

My first day was hard. I bravely marched into my first class and tried hard to fit in. I hadn't even taken any college prep courses. Going to college was never a dream of mine. I survived the first few weeks and was beginning to get the hang of college life. I made some friends and studied hard. In the evenings I did my assignments, and Jerome was also busy with his studies down at the technical school in Dayton. Mom was even starting to go out with some friends. Life was going smooth.

I was still a very timid and shy girl, and unfortunately after one of my speech classes, the professor mentioned he noticed I had a stutter and a lisp. If only I was able to have some counseling for my insecurity, I might have succeeded. But this made me even more embarrassed and I wanted to run and hide. There was no way I was strong enough to deal with this issue. Every time I would try to talk, I became a tongue-tied, babbling idiot. The instructor would make me practice in front of a mirror and I wanted to die. Most of my classmates were in all my other classes. We would have to prepare speeches and get up in front of the class and speak. I couldn't do it. I would try and just stammered and stuttered as I could

feel the class staring at me. I became more withdrawn and depression set in. Just the fear alone paralyzed me. I quit.

My parents were caught up in their own messes, so I just became more buried in mine. So what do you think happened next? You got it. That knight in shining armor came to rescue me. Not really but Jerome did step up to become the strong one. In reality that was the last thing I needed. Jerome had a controlling personality, so when I would find comfort under his wing, so to speak, he loved it. It kept me dependent on him. So while he continued to study during the week in Dayton, he would travel back to Canton for the weekends. During the weekdays, I stayed home with Mom.

I went and got a job at the hospital as a physical therapist aide. I loved it. I worked week days and had weekends off. Jerome continued to drive up every weekend to visit. Mom was not happy at all. She hated Jerome more than ever. She would do everything in her power to keep us apart. The more my mom and I would argue, I would grow more attached to him. He protected me. I never saw real love between my parents and I thought this was love between Jerome and I. I didn't know the difference. Since Dad was possessive of Mom, it seemed normal to have Jerome possessive of me.

The next few months I kept busy working hard at the hospital and found that I truly enjoyed patient care. You did not need a license certification to be an assistant as you do today. I enjoyed helping the therapist with treatments and working with the Hubbard tank. This is a huge tank that holds water with whirlpool motors

on the corners. The water therapy is soothing for stroke patients as well as burn patients. The gentle agitation helps to remove the dead skin.

My first burn patient was a young man named Gary. He had been in a horrific train/car collision, which killed his girlfriend. It left him with burns over 50 percent of his body. We were close to the same age so it became extremely hard to hear his screams and going through all the pain and agony. His legs were burned the worst as well as his hands. Although he had already lost several fingers, they were trying desperately to save his legs. They were so bad, mostly raw burned muscle and bone.

They always scheduled his whirlpool treatments and therapy after lunch. I must admit that some lunches were hard to swallow just knowing that I would soon be working with Gary. He was very pleasant and had dark-brown hair, once it grew back, as well as gorgeous dark-brown eyes. After they transported him down to me on a gurney, my job was to remove the bandages. I also removed some of his dead skin to help avoid any infection. Then I would lower him into the tank to allow him to soak with the gentle agitation of the whirlpool.

The next few months, it was amazing to see how well the skin grafts had healed, and actually his legs were looking so much better. It was time to start his physical therapy to strengthen his legs preparing him to walk again.

Within a few weeks we were wheeling him down the hall, saying our good-byes and well wishes. He was going home. Although I was so happy for Gary, I was going to miss him.

It was great to assist these people and watch them recover with their treatments. I got along well with my coworkers and loved going to work. But going home every evening to Mom was getting harder to cope with. She wouldn't let me leave the house, and we would literally get into a physical altercation if I tried to go somewhere. This made Jerome even more protective of me and we became engaged. He wanted to get me away from her and I was ready to leave. We planned a small wedding in June, during his break from school.

Dayton Bound

Trust in the Lord and do good; dwell in the land
and enjoy safe pasture. Take delight in the Lord,
and he will give you the desires of your heart.

Psalm 37: 3–4

We planned a small wedding at the church I went
to. I chose the color yellow for my bridesmaid's
dresses. My long time friend Shirley would be my maid
of honor. I had four friends be the bridesmaids and
Jerome's little sister Joyce was our junior bridesmaid.
Jennifer, Jerome's sweet little three-year-old sister, was
our flower girl. As much as I would have loved to have
my brother, Joey, there, he was stationed in Puerto Rico.
Jerome had his best friend as best man and four of his
friends as ushers, including his younger brother Jeff.

I found a beautiful white long gown with a pearl
bodice. My dad agreed to pay for the photographer.
We used the church hall for our reception and women
from the church volunteered to serve. Our cake was two
tiered and decorated with white and yellow roses. I had
just turned nineteen a couple weeks before, and Jerome
was turning nineteen the week after our wedding. Other

than Mom and I fighting before I left to go to the church to get married, as she was putting the guilt trip on me, everything went smoothly. Dad walked me down the aisle. We are now married. The reception was small but enjoyable. Since my parents are divorced, Dad's relatives were there but everyone seemed cold. Afterward we left for our honeymoon. We went to Cedar Point amusement park for a few days.

After our honeymoon was over, we headed down to Dayton to start our married life. I sadly left my job at the hospital and Jerome had a full-time job at a grocery store near our apartment building. Jerome didn't have many friends and I knew no one. The first week went well since I was busy making our place into our new home. I unpacked our wedding gifts and found a home for everything. Our apartment was a newly built one-room place. Jerome's grandparents gave us used furniture as well as a brand-new bed. We had everything we needed.

Jerome worked midnights so I tried to keep quiet during the day. We only had one car, but I didn't know my way around well enough to drive. It was pretty lonely, and once again, this shy girl felt backward and all alone. Sometimes I would hear noise in the bedroom thinking Jerome was getting up. I would run in to see him and that made him mad. I usually sat around watching the television. We were only married a few weeks when Jerome started pushing me around and hitting me. I was so devastated. I couldn't call Mom since I was too proud to admit she was right about him. I put my application at the hospital but had no response. I did get a job at a fast-food restaurant. That helped keep me busy and I was able to see people.

We never spoke about this, but after Jerome and I were married, he never went back to the technical school. There really was no reason for us to live down here. Jerome could have gotten a job in Canton. I could have kept my great job working in physical therapy.

After a few months of marriage, Jerome hurt his back. His mom—yes, his mom—scheduled an appointment with an orthopedic surgeon up in Canton. We made the trip there and it was determined that he had a ruptured disc. They wanted him to try traction first, but the doctor felt he would probably need surgery.

The day before he was to be admitted, Jerome hitchhiked up to Canton so I could have the car for work. That was ridiculous to me since I felt he could have been treated down here. Besides, my job wasn't that important to make me stay down here while my husband was hospitalized up in Canton. But Jerome was stubborn and I had no say in the matter. He left for Canton and I did everything I could to keep my mind occupied. I didn't have many friends and it just got so lonely. I started to get upset. Most people would have just gotten into the car and drove up, but I was always given the mindset that I was incapable. I called my mom and told her I wanted to come to Canton. When Jerome finally arrived in Canton after hitchhiking for five hours, Mom called him and asked him to drive back with a friend to get me. So even though he has pains shooting down his leg due to the ruptured disc, he and a friend drove back down the three hours it takes to get to Dayton. Then we drove back up to Canton, taking another three hours. We arrived back in time for him to be admitted in the

hospital. I know, mature people would have done things much differently, but we were only kids. The traction did not work so he had the surgery, and after a few weeks of recovering, we headed back to Dayton.

As he was recovering, I was hired in at the hospital as a cardiac technician trainee. I loved working at the hospital again. I worked on the step down unit from coronary care. I worked another year until we found out we were expecting our first baby.

Of course once again, we didn't make the best choice. We quit our jobs and moved back to Canton. Yes, that means we now no longer had insurance, and a baby was on the way.

Silent Night and Ashes

The Lord is my light and my salvation—whom
shall I fear? The Lord is the stronghold of my
life—of whom shall I be afraid?

Psalm 27: 1

After settling back in Canton, we purchased a new
mobile home located in this great allotment with
a clubhouse and pool. Jerome had gotten a job as a tool
and die designer even though he never finished his
school. It was Christmas time and I was four months
along with the baby. I had gotten a part-time job at a
department store.

It was Christmas Eve and I was so excited. My
brother, his wife, and their baby son were coming home
since his time in the service was completed. I hadn't seen
him for a couple of years. Jerome and I were leaving to
go to the midnight Christmas Eve service at church and
heard that Joey was planning on meeting us there. The
church was decorated with bright red poinsettias and
everyone was holding a burning candle. It was a night I
will never forget. Everyone was singing "Silent Night,"

and I turned around and saw Joey coming down the aisle behind me. Every time I hear that song I can't help but cherish that memory. I was happy and expecting our first baby and my brother was singing behind me. It was going to be a great Christmas. After the service, I happily hugged my brother and left that evening with plans to see them the next day.

I just remembered I forgot to mention something important. About a year ago, while Jerome and I were living in Dayton, my mom and dad married each other again. Yes, you heard it. I know, I thought the same thing.

Christmas afternoon Joey and his family came to our parents' house for dinner. We opened our gifts first since Dad had to work afternoons and would leave right after we ate. Everyone had a good time and I enjoyed holding my baby nephew, Dwayne. Dad left for work, and soon Joey and his family left to visit his wife's family. Jerome and I stayed a little while longer visiting with Mom. As we were getting ready to leave, I saw the candle burning on her table and I blew it out.

Jerome and I went home and we were getting ready for bed when the phone rang. It was my mom's neighbor calling to say Mom's house was on fire. Oh no. Jerome and I went to Mom's house as quickly as we could. As we pulled into the driveway, I saw fire trucks everywhere. The glow of their flashing lights reflected against the firemen working diligently to extinguish the fire. I could see the ambulance paramedics carrying out a stretcher from the house. I screamed for my mom as I ran to the back of the ambulance. Mom was covered in soot but she was alive. The fire had knocked out the electricity

and everything was dark. We followed the ambulance to the hospital as the firemen continued to put out the fire.

At the hospital while they were examining Mom, I called my brother to let him know, and then I called my dad at work.

"Can I talk to Joe Kornish, please?"

"Hello," said Dad.

"Dad, your house is on fire, and Mom is here at the hospital! You need to come home quickly!"

"I can't leave now!" Dad exclaims.

My dad said he could not leave work, even though I explained how their house was burning and Mom was in the hospital. It didn't seem to bother him. My brother arrived just when the doctors were releasing Mom. They said she was okay and she could go home. Right! I could not believe they were releasing her. Her hair was burnt and her face was blistered; she was still gasping for air.

My brother, Jerome, and I left the hospital with Mom, who was panicking and in shock. We were not sure what to do, where to take her. She started having trouble getting her breath and would attempt to open the car door and run. She was in shock. We took her back to the hospital and this time they admitted her. Her lungs were scorched. My little one hundred-pound mom had carried out all my brother's boxes of stuff, which he brought home from the service. She evidently made many trips into the burning house. This was a brick ranch and the fire had started behind the couch in the living room. So the living room and kitchen was destroyed and the rest of the house was heavily smoke damaged. The cause of fire was electrical.

Mom was hospitalized for nearly two weeks. After she was released, Jerome and I decided to bring her to our home to stay with us. Dad stayed in the basement of their burned house. They were soon able to move into an apartment till the house was remodeled. That was a good thing since Mom and Jerome do not, let me say it again, do not like each other.

The Blue Bundles

Children are a heritage from the Lord, offspring
a reward from him. Like arrows in the hands of a
warrior, are children born in one's youth.

Psalm 127: 3

After about eight hours of labor on May 30, 1973,
Jason Allen Thompson was born. We brought the
baby home and started our life as a family. It sure wasn't
easy. I knew that a new baby is expensive. We were
lucky to have relatives who gave us hand-me-down baby
clothes. Jason was a good baby and we were blessed with
a healthy son.

When Jason was four months old, Jerome was hired
as a policeman for the city of Canton. Jerome's father
had been on the force and he wanted to follow his father.
I didn't care if that was what he wanted to do except that
he would be making less money now as a cop.

About this time in our life, I found out I was three
months pregnant. Yes, Jason was only four months old.
Unbelievable but true. I was in shock to say the least.
Jerome didn't say much. He was still excited from
becoming a policeman. I just tried to imagine caring for

two babies less than one year old. I decided it was what it was and I would make the best of it. I started getting excited at each monthly checkup. When I went in for the fourth month, the doctor examined me and then stepped out of the room. He came back in with another doctor who then examined me.

"We are sorry to tell you but there is no baby."

"What do you mean there is no baby? Last month I heard the heartbeat!"

They shrugged their shoulders and sadly said again, "There is no baby in you."

My eyes welled up with tears; I felt so confused. They said they would perform an ultrasound.

They did an ultrasound and verified that there was no baby. I cannot tell you the emotions that went through me then. I felt confusion, sadness, and just so weird. I had not bled and there were no signs of any problems.

"Where did it go?" I asked. "What happened to the baby?"

They called it a missed abortion. It is when a woman's body absorbs the baby and tissues into her system. Evidently the baby had stopped growing and something must have been wrong with the baby, and it was nature's way of taking care of the problem. If I hadn't had a period the following month, I was to come in for a D and C. The next month my period started and all was well. Just hard to explain to people when they asked about my pregnancy. But after I settled down emotionally, I realized this was probably a blessing since Jason was still a young baby.

A couple years later, Jerome wanted another baby. Jason was two and a half years old when baby boy

number 2 was born. Christopher Michael Thompson was born on December 21, 1975. The doctors released me to take the baby home on Christmas Eve. We lived so close to the hospital at this time that I could see the roof of our home from my hospital room. I called Jerome and told him to come and get me. I was so anxious to see Jason again and bring the baby home. It actually took Jerome several hours to come and get me. I was so hurt. It was Christmas Eve and I had to sit in the hospital and wait. That was typical of Jerome. He was always so cold. We finally got home and I was so excited to introduce Jason to his new baby brother. I had heard that it helps siblings to bond if you bring the older child a gift from the baby. When Jason was looking at his new brother, we handed him a present, which we told him the baby had brought for him. Jason was delighted when he saw the stuffed toy monkey. He actually carried that monkey around for years.

Our life continued to be stressful. Jerome was always depressed and blamed me for everything that went wrong. I had my two healthy sons and that made me happy. I focused my attention on being the best mom and kept trying to be a loving wife. Jerome continued to be possessive and never liked any of my friends, so I usually stayed at home. He didn't like to have company over and was especially jealous of my brother. He always claimed that my brother's children were a bad influence on our kids. He would not let them around our boys. If it happened to be during the holidays, I had to check with Mom to see when Joey and his family were going so we would not come at the same time. This broke my

heart as well as Joey's. Jerome was mean and abusive, so I did what he said. I knew the consequences oh so well if I didn't. This kept me under his control, and once again, I hid in my shell. If I ever tried to get strong, he would knock me back down. We tried marriage counseling, but Jerome did not like hearing what they suggested, so he would quit going. Over the years I went to therapy myself just to keep my head above water and out of depression.

I tried doing my artwork and help make some extra money selling my paintings at craft shows, but since he was so jealous, he hated it when people talked to me. He would sit there and glare at my customers. I was never allowed to do the shows by myself. I gave up painting for many years since he didn't want me to paint. I was brainwashed and married to a man who carried a gun (policeman) didn't help. Cops are trained to argue and they have this attitude when they wear that uniform—they have power. I had no choice other than to be quiet, raise my boys, and keep everyone happy. I didn't matter and I had no value. I kept going to counseling and that helped keep me sane for a few more years.

Called to Say I Love You

> This is how we know what love is: Jesus Christ
> laid down his life for us. And we ought to lay
> down our lives for our brothers and sisters.
>
> 1 John 3: 16

Life went on. The boys were growing up and now busy with sports. I worked some part-time jobs to help ends meet, and Jerome continued being a grumpy, depressed man. He was who he was. He was always sick, missed a lot of work from stomach problems and high blood pressure. He gained a lot of weight over the years, especially since he had the back surgery. My mom was always ill also, many surgeries and back problems. Dad was still dad, working hard, still mean and abusive toward Mom, and he still kept her under his control. My brother had four kids and was very busy. He worked full time at the steel mill and part time at the hospital. He loved his kids and often took them with him if he was doing errands. I still never saw him or his family. It just caused too many problems between Jerome and me. It was easier to live lonely and sad than to make him mad. After all, I still had my hope to spend time with Joey in the future.

On April 22, 1983, after dinner, our phone rang. Jerome answered it and I knew something was wrong by the tone in his voice. While he was talking to the people on the phone, I asked him quietly, "My mom?" He shook his head no. Was it my dad? He again shook his head no. It must be someone in his family, so I went on cleaning up the dishes. He hung up the phone and he told me that my brother was dead.

"What? Joey is dead?"

"Was he in a car accident?" I cried out.

"They think he had a heart attack," Jerome said.

"Where is Mom? Does she know?"

Jerome told me that Mom and Dad were told and were on their way. It was Joey's wife who had called us. Stunned and in shock we hurried and dropped the boys off at Jerome's mom's house on the way. I had to get to my mom. She could not handle this. I ran inside and found her and Dad and Joey's kids. Debbie, Joey's wife, was in the room with Joey. Joey was only thirty-four years old. I could not believe this. He was a healthy nonsmoker.

As we sat in the little room, I found out that Joey had been mowing some elderly folk's lawn and wasn't feeling well and they left to go home. He had his eleven-year-old son and five–year-old daughter with him. They said their dad pulled off to the side of the road and fell over. They could not get a response from him. This was around eight thirty in the evening and it was dark. We figured it must have taken nearly a half an hour before the kids could get someone to stop and help them. A young couple did stop and was able to get Joey's lifeless body out of the car and into their car. They rushed Joey

and the kids to the hospital. We were never able to thank these kind folks. They left before anyone could meet them. They were angels to stop and help Joey's children during that horrific ordeal.

This was the hospital where Joey worked part-time as a phlebotomist. The staff knew Joey and started hard trying to save him. It was too late. Everyone was crying—the staff, his family, my parents. This could not be happening. It couldn't be, but it was. They took us back to see him. He was on a gurney with a surgical green cloth draping over him. They had opened his chest and tried to manually pump his heart. The doctors and coworkers loved him. They did all they could do to revive him. What are we going to do now?

My heart was so broken. I had to be strong for my mom. If only I had known God back then like I do now, but I didn't. As I write this, the memory of that night is still so painful.

We realized we didn't even know where Joey's car was. Jerome and the police department cruisers drove around for quite a while till they located the car. Jerome had one of the policeman drive the car to our home. The car still had the lawn mower inside along with bags of grass and leaves. An autopsy was performed and it was determined that Joey died from an aorta aneurysm. He had been having symptoms of a lower backache and hiatal hernia. Other than that he had seemed to be doing well.

The night before Joey passed, he had called my mom. She said they talked about his work and he told her he was just thinking that people are born and then they

die. There is not much in between. Then he must have noticed the time and told her, "I have to go. I just called to tell you I love you. Good-bye, Mom." The ironic thing is that Stevie Wonder came out soon afterward with that song, "I Just Called to Say I love You." Every time I heard it, which was quite often, I cried. I stayed with Mom for several days after Joey passed. I wanted to try to relieve her pain and to comfort her the best I knew how. The arrangements were made.

We drove my parents to the calling hours. We went over to his casket. I still could not believe he was gone. He looked so peaceful, like he was sleeping. I supported Mom as she looked down at her son. Her tears just flowed from her broken heart. We always hear this and it is so true. No parent should ever have to bury their children.

Joey knew so many people. People were lined outside the funeral home to pay their respect. It was such a shock to everyone. Joey's wife's mom had passed away only four months before. In fact, Joey was the executer of her mom's estate. Joey was the strong one, taking care of everyone else. He did so much for everyone he knew. It was hard. There were so many people that we had to schedule four different showings.

All this attention to my family was making Jerome upset. In between the calling hours, he would break my heart from all the mean things he would say. When it came time to decide who would ride in the family limousine to the grave site, I said I wanted to ride with the family. He stood outside arguing with me, mad since I didn't want to ride with him. I wanted to hold

Joey's youngest son who was only eighteen months old. Jerome kept yelling that I really wished it was him who died instead of my brother. What the heck? He was determined to make my life even more miserable than it was. I fought for this one. Yes, I did ride with the family to the grave site. It was my right as the only sister. And no one was going to take that away.

We buried Joey and life was going to be forever different. Debbie would have to find a way to survive with their four children without their father. I am proud to say, Debbie went to school and became a registered nurse and did a fine job raising her children. It wasn't easy and they dearly missed Joey in their lives. I am going to jump forward and tell you where they are today. All three sons went to school and are engineers, and the only girl went on to become a registered nurse herself. I know that Joey is looking down and smiling so proud. Debbie later married a nice man who loves them all very much. Debbie works at the same hospital where Joey had worked.

The Christmas before Joey passed, I made arrangements for Jerome and his siblings to have a family portrait done as a gift to their parents. Jerome was the oldest child, so being his wife, I always took on the job of getting the Christmas present. Jerome's brother lived in another state, so getting them all together was a challenge. But we succeeded and the picture came out great. I knew his mom would cherish a picture of all her four children together. This would be the perfect gift.

I wanted to have a portrait done of my brother and I for my parents too. Jerome said no. We would do it next

year. So now Joey is gone and I didn't have the picture. I was so hurt and felt angry but I am determined somehow, someway I would get this portrait done. I called a lot of photographers and they said I could have a picture of myself holding a picture of Joey. No way. I knew Joey was gone and I did not want a picture, which verified that. I just kept calling more photographers until I did find a way to do it. This glorious photographer asked if I could find a recent picture of my brother. I was thrilled when Debbie told me about the proofs she had from Akron University. They were photos taken for his student passes. The photographer had me pose with the same lighting they had used for Joey's picture. I wore an outfit that coordinated with his burgundy jacket. After that picture was ready, they were able to combine the pictures side by side as if they were taken at the same time. They did some airbrush touchups to blend them together. The portrait turned out magnificent. This was a very expensive project but I did have my picture with Joey and I together. It made this sad Christmas a little brighter to have this picture a reality. My parents proudly hung the picture up in their living room.

When I would hear my treasured Christmas song, "Silent Night," I would break down in tears. The memory of that special Christmas Eve when I saw Joey for the first time after all those years broke my heart now.

As far as my life, what can I say? I became very angry after my brother passed. I missed a lot of life we could have spent together. I missed so much of him, of knowing him and just being his sister. I miss Joey. I was angry for Jerome for taking that part away from me that

I can never get back. I continued to be there for Mom and help her grieve. As far as my dad, you know, when we were at the calling hours, someone mentioned to me privately that this might be a good time to get close to my dad. I actually went up to my dad, put my arms around him to hug him, and he shoved me away. That really broke my heart. Especially when I hear friends talk about being their daddy's girl. He never showed any emotion. He was just cold. Jerome never changed, was still possessive and controlling.

Jerome and I planned on going to the policemen's ball. I wanted it to be special, so I picked out a pretty dress. I fixed my hair and I felt I looked pretty good. After we got to the dance, Jerome walked up to me and asked me why I wore that dress and how I looked terrible in it. There I was, Ms. Shrinking Violet, I could have crawled in a hole if I could have found one. I wanted to hide and that was exactly what he wanted. It took me many years to realize he was so insecure himself that he felt powerful making us feel bad. If we went anywhere as a family, he would yell at the boys and about how bad they looked. We never had a good relaxed time. He always ruined it for us. He was abusive towards the boys also, especially Jason. Jason would always work so hard around the house doing chores, but they were never done the right way or at least the way Jerome thought they should be done.

It took me a long time to realize that it wasn't me. Jerome was so unhappy that he didn't want anyone else to be happy. He always wanted to buy things, temporary fixes for his depression. He bought a motorcycle, fishing

boat, had a swimming pool installed, and anything else he could put on the charge card. You know, buying these big toys never made him happy. We just got deeper in debt. More stress for a dysfunctional family. I hung in there, just kept dragging more stuff behind. Writing this at this time in my life has been very emotional. Joey has been gone twenty-nine years now. My heart is still broken and I miss him so much. Someday we will be together again.

It was about this time in my life when Henry arrived. Sweet Henry was such a blessing to me. He called where I worked looking for someone who might do some artwork for him. That was how I met Henry Ringer. Okay, right now you are thinking, "Sally is about to have an affair," aren't you? Get those nasty thoughts out of your head. When I met Henry, he was ninety years old. I might have run away with him if he was fifty years younger—he was so sweet. There are people that you know God brought into your life like a guardian angel. Henry was mine.

Henry had worked for Henry Ford—yes, the real Henry Ford. He worked as an engineer and was quite a good designer and craftsman. He didn't start his wind machine business till after his wife died. She didn't want any sawdust in her house. Henry and I started our partnership when he was ninety.

Henry would design these wind machines on paper. They were very detailed with many working gears that in turn made the figures move. A large propeller would spin in the wind, or else you could manually turn it, and this activated the gears. Then the gears would move

wired objects to put things in motion. He would carve out the bodies, arms, legs out of wood. These designs were incredible. He had lawyers, dentists, teachers, brick layers, and many, many more. He would get an order from a customer and design what they wanted. First he would draw it out on paper, gears and all the moving parts. He would take a block of wood and carve out the parts that would move. That is where I came in. He would give me a paper telling me which colors he wanted me to paint the figures.

By now his handwriting was so shaky, very hard to read. I was always amazed how he was able to work with his bent, arthritic fingers. My artwork brought the wood sculptures to life. After I finished painting the items, we would put them together.

Henry was my sanity during this sad time in my life. When he called at work he would always ask to speak to Ms. Sally. He was such a delightful man with the kindest heart. He was always positive and made me feel good when we were together. He knew that Jerome was controlling and that my life was depressing. When I came to see him, he always had his old *Guidepost* magazines to give me and his encouragement kept me going.

Henry and I continued our business partnership for the next ten years. When Henry turned a hundred years old, he surprised me with my own wind machine he had built. It is a girl painting, and she turns side by side, moving her paintbrush up and down on a wood canvas. I will always cherish my special wind machine. That was the last wind machine we made. Not long after, Henry fell and broke his hip. He passed away several

months later. At his funeral, I cried so hard. I had lost my best friend who believed in me. Henry and I made over seventy-five wind machines over a period of ten years together. I loved Henry. He gave me the special gift of my wind machine, but in reality, he was the best gift of all.

Full Moon

Take delight in the Lord, and he will give you the desires of your heart. Commit your way to the Lord; trust in him and he will do this.

Psalm 37:4–5

After my brother died, I could feel him in my heart. I would talk to Joey since he was now part of me, always with me and in my heart. My brother was a very special man. His life was about giving to others. He always had a kind word to say or would come to the help of a friend in need. He accomplished so much in his thirty-four years. I always wanted to be like him; I always admired him. Since he passed away, I often gazed up to the stars on a clear night. I knew he was in heaven and felt he was one of those bright shining stars watching over us. When there was a full moon, I couldn't get him out of my mind. Memories would drift into my thoughts. I missed him so much.

One evening late at night during a glorious full moon, I felt God tugging on my heart. The moonlight was so bright that my bedroom had a special glow. Jerome was working the midnight shift and the boys were already fast asleep. I had heard that the only way to heaven was through Jesus. When you surrender yourself to our Savior, you would be saved. It was dark in my bedroom except for the glow of that moon. I climbed up on the bed and I cried out to the Lord. Please, Jesus, I want to be saved. I reached my arms high up toward the ceiling and I cried out. I have heard that people would fall over and pass out. I also heard that people's lives would be forever changed during that moment. Nothing seemed to happen to me. But somehow I knew deep in my heart that Jesus heard me. I wondered if I would even remember this night. Although through the years my life never changed too much since I was basically surviving, but as I write this story some twenty-nine years later, I do remember that evening as if it was last night. I also know that God has been here through all my pain. I just didn't know how to find help. If I tried, the people in my life would not allow me to get stronger. They liked me weak and under their control. That was how I lived and I didn't know any better.

The Accident

May the God of hope fill you with all joy and peace as you trust in him, so that you may overflow with hope by the power of the Holy Spirit.

Romans 15: 13

My sons had grown up so much. Jason has signed up early for the navy during his senior year. He would be leaving for boot camp soon after his high school graduation. Chris and Jason were both very much involved with the Boy Scouts. I was very proud of their determination to both become Eagle scouts.

I started my day early on March 13, 1991. I was meeting Jerome up in Akron after I got off work that afternoon. Jerome was already at the workman's compensation meeting at Quaker Square. I had a lot to do verifying the plans for the boys and making sure they had food to eat. I would not be coming back home till the next day. I went to work knowing I had everything prepared.

Walking out to my car after work, I was excited about my drive to Akron. I never drove out of Canton before and was a little nervous. I proudly pulled into the parking lot of Quaker Square. Jerome was waiting when I arrived. After taking my suitcase up to the room, we went down to the restaurant and had a nice dinner. Afterward we decided to check out the quaint shops inside of Quaker Square. This building used to house the Quaker Square Company in the olden days. They have since turned the large silos into gorgeous hotel accommodations. And there are many quaint shops throughout this facility.

I wanted to find a candle and a candleholder. I looked around for some time until I found the perfect holder. Then I had to smell the candles till I found the one I wanted. Jerome wanted me to get a Precious Moment figurine to keep as a memory of this trip. I had a large collection already so finding that special one took a while, but I found a pretty one.

We went up to our room and I wanted to light my candle. It smelled so good and I enjoyed sitting there quietly watching the candlelight flicker. It was such a peaceful moment.

The phone rang. Who could that be? I answered it and it was one of Jerome's policeman friends. I handed the phone to Jerome wondering what this guy could possibly want. Then I overheard Jerome say, yes, our son was going to ride with a friend to the scout meeting. What? Where? At this point I was becoming very nervous. Jerome told the guy on the phone that we would be right there as he hung up the phone. Jerome said that Chris was in an accident and was at the hospital. I got the impression it must be a broken leg or something like that. I hesitated whether I should pack up my stuff.

Were we coming back? I didn't know. So we decided to pack it all up and ran out to Jerome's truck. Usually it would take twenty minutes to drive that distance, but we were there in ten minutes. While Jerome was parking near the trauma center entrance, I ran inside. Right away someone approached me and asked if I was Mrs. Thompson.

"Yes, I am," I said.

"Come with me."

They took me into a room where some policemen had already gathered. Soon Jerome ran in and I could hear all kinds of comments like, his legs were moving, they didn't think he was paralyzed, etc. A nurse came over and said a doctor left an order if I needed something to help me to relax.

"What? Where is Chris?" I cried out.

"They are treating his injuries. We will take you back to see him soon."

"What happened?" My voice quivered as I tried to speak.

We were told bits and pieces of the accident. Our fifteen-year-old son, Chris, was on his way home from Boy Scouts with three other boys in his troop when the driver lost control of the car. Just moments before, Chris has unfastened his seatbelt to lean forward to talk to his friend sitting in the front seat. The car lost control and went end over end up a hill and flipped, overthrowing Chris out the back window. The car rolled over on Chris. The other boys had their seatbelts on during the accident. They had minor cuts and bruises. My head was spinning. I was trying to understand but everything

was happening so fast. I was feeling sick. I wanted to see Chris.

The trauma doctor walked in and wanted to talk to us. He explained that Chris had many serious injuries, and after they do the CT scan, they would know more. They said we could see him briefly before they took him down for the scan.

The room was buzzing with nurses, doctors, technicians, and people working all around him. I could see Chris. He was unconscious. His head was so swollen and it didn't even look like him. He had blood coming out his eyes, ears, and mouth. There was a bloody neck collar on the floor. Machines were beeping and there were wires and tubes everywhere. I felt so numb and scared. This was my boy, my baby boy. He was breathing with the help of machines. My voice was quivering as I told him we were there and that we loved him. They took us to another room to wait while they took Chris for the CT scan.

It had been over an hour, which seemed like eternity, until the doctor came in with the prognosis. Chris had four skull fractures, twelve facial fractures, and his brain was severely damaged. His pelvis was in three pieces. His jaw was broken in several places and he had lost his front teeth. He may not recover, and if he did, they weren't sure to what extent of damage he had to his brain. He had massive internal bleeding caused by a facial fracture, which nicked his carotid artery. The internal bleeding was causing his eye to protrude. They said there was nothing they could do at this point except to keep him comfortable. Every hour he lived was in his favor. I was

just in shock and numb, shaken beyond belief. I was in so much shock, I actually did not cry.

All of a sudden it came to me. The night before, I had both my teenage sons sit down and watch a rerun of a television show I had seen in the past. It was an episode of *911* showing a couple cars loaded with teenagers having some harmless fun. But it turned into a disaster. The one car was chasing the other and it lost control and flipped over, throwing one of the boys out. I am now realizing that God had showed me a preview of my life and what was to happen. It showed procedures and explained to me what they were doing to my son. So whatever they were doing to Chris, I recalled the scene from the television show to what had been done to the boy then. I knew exactly what was happening. The boy had similar injuries. While watching the show, Chris had even asked why this boy was hurt so bad. I explained that he did not have his seatbelt on.

The boy on the show did recover after many surgeries and lots of therapy. To my amazement, his name was also Chris. His hair was even blond like my son's hair. His mother had written a daily journal on her son's recovery. So I decided to do the same. This gave me hope.

Jerome had called his parents and family members and they all came in. My parents were ill and elderly. I felt it was better not to tell them yet. I called my friend and her husband and they quickly arrived to give me some support. After I told my friend how serious Chris's condition was, her husband suggested we go to the chapel in the hospital to pray.

I will be forever grateful to my friends. I was in no condition to get there by myself. I remember looking up at the beautiful statue of Jesus as I gave Chris to the Lord. I put everything into God's hands. As I prayed for strength, I knew that God's will would be done. Something amazing happened. I suddenly felt such an inner peace. I knew God was there with me. God told me that Chris was going to live. It would be a long road ahead, but he would recover. I can't explain it, except it was God.

After we returned from the chapel, Chris was moved into the Intensive Care Unit. Because of all his massive head injuries, he began to convulse. Jerome, Jason, and Chris's grandfather were there by his side, trying desperately to restrain him from banging his head. The emotional stress was causing Jerome to become ill. They took Jerome down to ER to examine him. He was soon admitted into Coronary Care. His blood pressure was extremely high and he had problems with his heart. They needed to keep an eye on him.

The next few days, Chris continued to hold his own although he still hadn't regained consciousness. I kept going from ICU to CCU. They kept Jerome sedated and put a hold on his visitors. All his policeman friends were concerned about his son therefore he could not rest.

It was very hectic. I spent most of my time with Chris and was concerned for Jason. Jerome's mom stepped in to make sure Jason's needs were being met. He only had a few months until he graduated and he would be leaving for the navy.

I hadn't been home for days and barely slept. I was told that the doctors were concerned that Chris's spleen might rupture. If it did, they had no choice but to rush him into surgery. He could die either way. They also found a tear in his bladder. The next few hours were critical. He had already received four units of blood.

Jerome's dad took me to the side and said we needed to start making funeral arrangements. I was so mad. No!

Then he said, "You do not realize how bad Chris is."

"I do. But we will handle what we have to handle when the time comes."

And as I walked away, he muttered, "You are in denial."

The next morning God gave me the best gift. When I went in to see Chris, the nurse was working on him, and when she saw me, she said, "Your mom is here, Chris. Let's show her what you can do." I was holding his hand and she told him to squeeze my hand. I felt a slight movement but was skeptical due to the involuntary reflexes due to the respirator. The nurse told Chris to move his big toe. It wiggled ever so slightly. The nurse then said, "Come on, Chris. Really show your mom what you can do." At that point Chris's foot started moving back and forth. The nurse and I cried with so much happiness. We now knew that Chris's brain was functioning. We had definite signs of hope. He was in there. The doctors told me how they were amazed with Chris and that he was definitely a fighter.

The next few days Chris started having miraculous recoveries. First his spleen had formed a pocket around itself and the bladder continued to heal on its own. The doctors had planned on putting pins into his broken

pelvis, but it was beginning to show signs that it was healing together. I wish I could put into words how I was feeling. The peace that God gave me, it was as if God was sitting on my shoulder. I must have shined with his glory. Being the mother of the youngest patient in ICU, the other patients and their families were always asking about Chris. They wanted to hug me and I always had a positive attitude, but then again, I knew that Chris was going to recover.

Jerome was released from CCU. We finally got to go home to shower and change. Oh, to be clean with fresh clothes on, but I needed to get back as soon as we could. I just could not stay away. We hurried back to be with our son.

Chris still could not see due to the massive swelling and bruising around his eyes. He could not speak because of the breathing tube in his mouth. He started to try to communicate with us by using his fingers to spell out words. His first question was. What happened? What happened to the other guys?

The next few days his vital signs began to stabilize so he was finally taken off the respirator. Speaking his first words, he told us how much he loved us and that he felt like he had been in a twilight zone. The doctors felt that he was stable enough to do the reconstructive facial surgery. They needed to repair the fractures with bone plates before the natural healing would start. They also needed to repair his broken jaw. They scheduled the surgery for the next morning.

I was sleeping on the couch in the ICU waiting room when I was awakened by Chris's nurse. Chris was

asking for me. It was around three in the morning. Chris began to tell me he saw the pictures. We had hung some posters up of a gulf war pilot giving the thumbs-up sign. But Chris hadn't regained his sight yet, so how could he see the posters?

Again he said, "I see the pictures."

"What pictures, Chris?"

He proceeded to tell me pictures of death. I quickly responded, "No, Chris, you are going to be okay."

Then he said, "No, mom, I'm not going to make it."

It took all my strength to keep from crying as I reassured him once again that he was going to be okay. Then he dozed off to sleep. During those next hours, I stayed by his side watching him sleeping so peacefully and hoping he was strong enough to survive the surgery. Even though I felt God's love and faith surrounding us, I was so scared and frightened.

In the morning, they came and took Chris to surgery. After seven long hours, it seemed like forever till the doctor called to let me know that Chris has come through the surgery just fine. But due to wiring his jaws shut, they had to perform a tracheotomy on him. All the fractures were set with bone plates.

When I got to see him they had a large ice bag wrapped around his face due to the swelling. My poor baby looked like a chipmunk. They kept him heavily sedated due to the pain. The next day he continued to recover well.

The day following he went downhill quick. He had a fever of 103 and it continued to rise. When your son is already at the best possible place for medical help and

the best medically trained people are doing all they can, you feel totally helpless. We had come so far, and after all their efforts, his temperature continued to rise to 104. They were covering him in ice blankets, antibiotics, and nothing was working. After an extremely tearful day, they were finally able to get the fever down. He had an infection in his lungs and the antibiotics were finally taking effect.

Although Chris was showing much improvement, the doctors were very concerned about what was going on behind his eye. I had no idea that he could still die due to the bleeding behind his eye. We would have to go to University hospital in Cleveland to have an embolization done. The doctors felt that Chris had improved enough where he could make the trip to Cleveland.

It took an hour by ambulance to transport Christ to University Hospital. The doctors met us there and explained the procedures they were planning. First they would go into the artery in the groin and perform an angiogram. That would determine the exact location of the damage in the carotid artery.

The angiogram went well and we were introduced to the doctor who would be doing the embolization. His name was Dr. Tarr and he looked a lot like Jesus with his long brown hair. There were only a few doctors specially trained in the world who could do this rare procedure. I was told that up to a few years ago, it could not have been done. They hadn't invented the complex flexible instruments required until then. So I felt very blessed that God directed us to this awesome doctor. We called him super doc.

The embolization, a very complex surgical procedure, was amazing. They would go through the artery in the groin with very pliable tubing and let it travel up to the carotid artery located behind the eye. There they would attempt to pace very tiny balloons, the size of pin heads, to block the flow of blood, which was rushing through this tear. Going through the artery in the groin on Chris's other side would be a tube with a camera so they can see what they were doing. Chris must lay still on his back, awake while they attempt this. We were informed of the risks of stroke or death if the balloons become dislodged during or after surgery. The situation would remain critical until the blood would clot around the repair. Signing those release papers for this risky surgery was terrifying. I actually got so dizzy I almost passed out. They scheduled the surgery the next day.

We were blessed that we had the opportunity to stay at the Ronald McDonald house. It was close enough where I could walk to the hospital. They provide housing for families of critically ill children at no cost to the family. This was our home away from home for nearly a month.

The embolization took ten hours and Chris did fine but they were not able to completely seal the tear. They would attempt it again with some tiny coils in a day or so. The second embolization was a success and it only took five hours. The tear was repaired and the bleeding had stopped. The next day the swelling in his right eye went down. After a few more days, they were able to wean him off the respirator. We were so relieved and totally exhausted. This was such an emotional ordeal.

The next concern was his eyesight. An eye doctor was sent in to examine Chris. Chris's optic nerve and the many nerves around his eye were damaged beyond repair. Chris would never regain his sight in his right eye. In fact, we were told he would probably never be able to open his eyelid. At this point I started getting greedy and wanted everything healed. I would push Chris around in his wheelchair and people would see him with his eye closed and think he was sleeping. I would turn him around so they could see his other eye open. I began to pray for his eye to open. Yes, you did hear me say pray. I had faith but still hadn't prayed that often.

Next they started working on his legs. The physical therapists worked with Chris to strengthen his leg muscles. He had muscle weakness due to the paralysis to his left side caused by the brain injury. Chris worked hard retraining those muscles so he could use his legs, just to learn to walk again. Three more weeks of intensive therapy and we were told we could go home.

We are finally on our way home to Canton. Yes, my miraculous son had overcome with God's healing. We still had a long road of therapy to conquer, but look how far Chris had come. It was so good to be home with Jason again. We had only several weeks left before Jason was to graduate. We had so much to catch up on.

It was also great to have Chris around his friends again and Jason. Chris was still using crutches to get around and adapting well to only having vision in his left eye. We continued with physical therapists and occupational therapists coming every day to work with Chris. Chris was still not able to talk since his jaws were

wired shut. He would write down his messages. Since he had missed so much school, we needed a tutor. We only had use of a school-provided tutor for two weeks since school would be out for the summer. There was so much homework to make up and adjusting with some headaches and his eyesight.

I am proud to say that Chris not only succeeded, he got all As. Chris has recovered all but his right eyesight. Yes, even his eyelid is open. And for a mother keeping a daily journal of her son's recovery, that is how I was able to write this story. I had kept great notes in my journal, the gratitude of a mother who watched her son recover from a near-death accident to see his miraculous recovery. I praise God every day. God told me he would be okay. In fact he is doing awesome.

Chris went on to become an Eagle Scout along with his brother, Jason. And I am going to brag that Chris even made the dean's list in college.

After Jason graduated from high school, he left two weeks later for boot camp. We tearfully drove him to Cleveland and left him with the other naval recruits waiting to fly to Florida. Jason left six days after Jerome and my twentieth wedding anniversary. Jason and I were always close as were Jerome and Chris, two of a kind. When Jason left, I lost my best buddy and I knew our family would never be the same again. I missed him so much after he left for the navy. I felt so alone.

That summer Chris continued to recover and Jerome became even more controlling. I gained a new strength watching Chris overcome his obstacles. I was not going to take it from Jerome anymore. I had had enough of his

possessiveness. I wanted a life. In August, after we came back from Jason's graduation from boot camp in Florida, I told Jerome I wanted out of the marriage.

When given the choice of which parent he wanted to stay with, Chris chose his dad. It broke my heart. I had already lived twenty years of abuse, and even if it meant I would have to live alone, I had to leave. I could have fought for the house, but Chris deserved to have his home. Several months later, we had gotten a dissolution of the marriage.

I found an apartment and Chris and I spent time together on the weekends. Yes, this was the worst year of my life, and to survive from drowning, sometimes you have to hurt those you love. I did not have anything left to give; I had given my all.

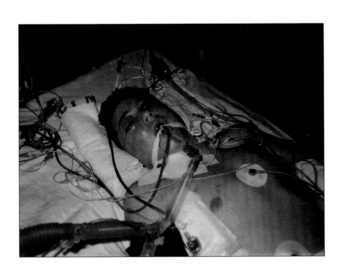

Red Dog Night

Then they cried out to the Lord in their trouble,
and he delivered them from distress.

Psalm 107: 6

When I found my unfurnished little cozy house to rent, I was so excited. It was so quaint and had cottage windows. It had a large kitchen, one bedroom, a little bathroom, a living room, and a stone fireplace. It was so cute and perfect for me. The problem was I didn't bring any furniture with me. I felt Chris had gone through hell with the accident and I wanted him to have his home left intact.

As soon as my friends and coworkers heard about my new place, they were happy to donate pieces for my home. Unbelievable but I had it completely furnished with all I needed by the end of the day. Someone had even given me a fold-out sleeper couch for Chris or Jason when they would come to visit. I could not believe the generosity of my friends. I was so excited turning this house into my home.

I had some old fabric and I made ruffled curtains for the windows. I made a cute skirt for the bathroom sink, which gave me some storage space under the skirt. It was so cute and charming. Jerome would never let me decorate. When I moved out, we still did not have any kitchen cupboard doors from the remodel he started eight years before. When my friends came to visit, they were happy to see that I had cupboard doors.

While married, if you recall, I was never allowed to go anywhere. He would never let me go for a walk. Guess what? My first day in my new home, I went to the city park and walked the walking path. It was like I was out of prison and saw freedom for the first time. I loved it. I started walking the path every day, then twice a day. Eventually I walked four and half miles a day, rain or shine. I lost the extra weight I put on without even trying. While walking the path, I could see the hospital where Chris was admitted that horrific night. I would count my blessings as I walked and walked. It was so awesome.

Chris started his junior year in school that fall and continued doing well. After a while I noticed that Chris was becoming cold toward me when I called. Later I found out that Jerome had been using Chris as his therapist. Jerome just kept complaining and putting me down. Chris was feeling angry since he had to deal with Jerome's negativity and depression. I became the blame for everything. I had always been the blame or excuse when Jerome was depressed all our married years. I was sad that Chris had to be put in that situation. But there was no way I would ever come back to Jerome.

Mom and Dad were having heart problems and they both had had open-heart surgery. I continued to be there when I could to make sure their needs were taken care

of. Dad still was abusive to Mom and there was nothing I could do. If I stepped in the middle, that caused more problems between them. Jason was on a ship stationed out in the Persian Gulf. It was great to hear from him when he would call home. If he got some time off on leave, he would come home to visit.

One night a friend who loved country music asked me if I wanted to go with her and her husband to see this country band. She told me it was at a saloon and I said no way. She convinced me that we were not going to be in the bar section. We would be enjoying this band and their music. The band was pretty good and folks were dancing and having a good time. The waitress came over to tell me that this guy wanted to buy me a drink. I told her I was drinking pop and she came back with my drink and a piece of paper with his phone number on it. I smiled at him and later went over to thank him. He had gone to the same high school I graduated from although I did not remember him. I did know his younger sister.

After I went home, my friend asked if I was going to call him. I told her no way, I was not calling some guy I met in a bar. By the way, the bar was called the Red Dog Saloon. She laughed and reminded me how cute he was. Four days later, I called him against any common sense I should have had. We talked for four hours. He was so easy to talk to and we continued to talk again for the next couple nights. We went out on a date, and afterward, he took me to visit his widowed mom. He was from a large family and I could tell he adored his mom.

After a few more dates, I took him up to visit my mom in the hospital. She was having more heart problems. My

mom liked him right away and he was so charming. He was a country fellow and wore country boots. He was very handsome although he was shorter than me. He was always laughing and he loved to sing. He was very romantic and would sing all the country songs to me.

His family was Italian/German and they were from the other side of the tracks, if you know what I mean. Hard and rough and used a lot of foul words. Now I am the sweet, shy, and quiet type and this was a big change for me. I should have run fast when I mentioned to him that I had lost forty pounds, especially when he said, "Oh yeah? You could stand to lose a few more pounds."

He was a charmer and convinced me to move in with him. I was enjoying this different life. He never abused me physically but I always felt like I wasn't up to his standards. He would tell me that he had dated so many women and not to worry when a girl would come up to hug him. Remember I was a shy and very insecure girl. This made me feel very inadequate. When we would be at the hospital visiting Mom during her hospital stays, he would say he dated a lot of these nurses. Of course every nurse that came in, I wondered if he dated her before. I tried to leave him many times, but being the charmer he was, he always knew how to sweet talk me back.

After we lived together for two years in his apartment, I purchased a charming Tudor-style house in the same neighborhood where we lived. My parents helped me with the down payment, so I didn't put his name on anything. After we moved in, he really became different. He didn't like my house, or maybe it was because he didn't have any control anymore. I had gotten a better job and

was working with the handicapped. From my younger days volunteering at the cerebral palsy camp, I had always wanted to work with disabled folks. So things were going my way. But he became more distant and we weren't getting along. I asked him to leave. He said he would look for a place, but after a few weeks, he was still there.

At that time, my mom was diagnosed with lung cancer. One evening after visiting my mom, I came home and he was downstairs in the family room watching the television. I sat down on the couch to relax. Pretty soon he ran over and jumped on me. I pushed him away and he went crazy. He grabbed me and we fell to the floor and we continued to wrestle. I kept fighting back trying to get away and he grabbed my hair and banged my head on the ground. I was seeing stars but kept trying to get away. By now he jumped on me and choked me by holding his thumbs on my throat. He always said he was a Green Beret in the army stationed in Vietnam. I think he was using some of those moves on me. I struggled and got away and grabbed the phone. He ripped the phone wires from the wall. Oh my, next thing I knew he had my hair in his hands and began banging my head on the floor again. I can remember being pinned down, and as I was looking up at the ceiling tiles, I knew I was going to die. All I could think about was my poor mom. How could she handle my death? How could I get away?

He got up and walked into the laundry room. I jumped up and tried to run up the stairs. It was too late, for he had walked out with a gun. He shoved me on the couch and proceeded to push the end of the barrel into my face. His eyes were mad, a look I never saw before. He glared at me.

I tried to reason with him but he was a crazy man. I cried and cried but he wouldn't put the gun down. He just kept shoving that gun in my nose. This was not happening, this had to be a bad dream, but it was real! This went on for hours. My face was bleeding from the deep scratches, and I could feel blood trickling down my cheek where he had pulled out my hair. I kept hoping he would come to his senses. He just kept talking craziness and glaring at me and the gun never seemed to move.

I started telling him how everything would be fine, we would be okay, just put the gun down. I told him I would stay with him. Then he slowly brought the gun down to his side. I got him to talk about his family, talk about anything just to distract him. Now it had been five hours since I came home. After I could see him calming down and breathing slower, I was able to talk him into going to bed. We went up to the bedroom and I went and lay down on the bed. He crawled in on his side of the bed. I stayed on my side and kept very still waiting for him to fall asleep. I heard his deep breathing and soon he started to snore. I crawled down off my side of the bed and crawled out into the hallway. I quietly grabbed my clothes I had worn earlier and went downstairs to dress. We didn't have a cell phone, and since the phone was destroyed, I needed to get to the nearest pay phone.

I drove my car down the street and pulled into a parking lot. I called the police and they met me at the parking lot by the pay phone. I told them what happened and they followed me and my car back to the house. I let them in and they went upstairs. With their guns pointed at him, they woke him up. They asked him where the

gun was and he told them. They retrieved the gun. They handcuffed him and took him to jail.

The police officers asked me to follow them downtown to the police station and make a police report. Then the detectives questioned me and took photographs of my injuries. I went to the hospital ER for treatment. Yes, I had a concussion, severe bruising on my throat along with deep scratches and bruises. I called off work and went to see my parents. I explained my injuries to them, and once again, they were older and confused, they didn't say much. I took Mom to her chemotherapy treatment. I finally had time to realize that I was alive and I had actually lived through that ordeal. Thank God.

I got a protection order and I had to go to court. His family came and moved all his stuff out of the house. He remained in jail for a few more days because of some outstanding arrest warrants. His sister bailed him out of jail. Once he was released I lived in fear. I was scared to death. A protection order is just a piece of paper. I had the locks changed on the house.

I went to work forever looking over and around my shoulder. The managers where I worked set up a code to follow in case he entered the building. My life was just so scary. I slept with my clothes on and one eye open. I continued to care for my mom and take her to her chemotherapy treatments.

This is where I get really confused. Truly my thoughts are a blur and I am not sure exactly what happened. I know one thing for sure. I was not of a sane mind. I had my phone number changed but somehow, someway, this guy got a hold of me. I will not ever use his name in this book. I will not tarnish my book by including his name.

I really want to forget it and since it is not necessary to this book, I won't disclose it.

We started talking on the phone again. Yes, this guy who just held a gun to my head. I think I was just so tired of running and hiding. He promised he would never hurt me again. Yes, and I wanted to believe him. Remember charmers know just what to say. I started making excuses to myself. It was my fault. Or it was Vietnam or Agent Orange, just crazy thinking. I will admit, I was not right in my thinking. After all, that crazy glare in his eyes before, I had never seen this before, he must have lost his mind as a result of the war. After all, he was now the nicest guy in the world. I was later reminded by a therapist that this was exactly what my parents had done. All this stupidity now made sense to me.

Guess what? I married him. Oh yeah, I am sure you are shaking your head now. So am I. And I decided if I never made him mad again, he would never hurt me. My parents didn't seem to care if we got married. But I had to hide it from my close friends. I knew they would think I was crazy and try to talk me out of it.

We went and met with the pastor at my church. He did not know anything about the gun situation. We took a pre-wedding test and the pastor said we scored the best of anyone who had taken the test before. He said we were definitely compatible. Before I walked down the aisle with him, my son Jason begged me not to do it. I made excuses to my son also, that it must have been post-traumatic war injury. We did get married in the church. You will find out later that we did not live happily ever after. The good thing is that I am still alive to be writing this book.

Saying Good-bye

> There is a time for everything, and a season for every activity under the heavens; a time to be born and a time to die, a time to plant and a time to uproot.
>
> Ecclesiastes 3: 1–2

A few days before we were married, my mom fell and broke her hip. One good thing I will admit was that he was fantastic with my parents. He really did show them compassion and was always such a great care giver. She needed surgery, but with her chemo and heart problems, she might not be strong enough to live through the operation. The surgeons said that she was in so much pain and could not survive without the surgery either. Her pelvis was broken so bad that her legs were going sideways. We decided to go with the surgery.

Saying good-bye as they wheeled her down the hall was so hard. Once again my tiny ninety-pound momma overcame the odds. She did fine. After a few days, she was then released from the hospital to a rehabilitation center for therapy. Recently my Mom had been showing signs of dementia and was very confused. She would walk with her walker behind her. The therapists and I struggled daily to help her understand to keep the walker in front of her as she walked.

One morning my dad came up to visit her and he had a dead mouse in his shirt pocket. He was so proud of it. He found it at home in a mouse trap. He was grinning ear to ear like a hunter who had just shot a big buck and had to show it off. I tried to take it from him, but he said he would throw it away when he went outside. That evening when he came back to see Mom, the mouse was still in the pocket. Oh yes, I took that mouse out of his pocket right then and there and flushed it down the toilet.

She was recovering and about to be released to go home. First we would need to arrange to have home health care. The visiting nurse would come every few days. We started noticing that Mom's prescriptions were getting all messed up. Dad had been hiding her prescription bottles. I worked during the day so I couldn't be there all the time. The nurse and I had to devise a way to handle this situation. I came before work and was there when she took her morning dose, and then I would count the pills in the separate pills boxes. Then after work I would make sure she took her evening pills. The nurse counted pills when she came. We kept the prescription bottles hidden away from Dad.

Mom continued her chemo another couple months. The doctor had her on a small dose, which didn't make her sick or lose her hair. The doctor and I agreed not to put her through any major life-saving treatments. It mainly kept her hopeful and she enjoyed visiting with

the other patients. We had meals on wheels to provide their lunch and dinner.

When Mom started getting weaker and lost more weight, we stopped the chemo. She was down to sixty pounds. She was more confused and didn't want to eat. Dad became more anxious trying to make her eat. That made Mom angry. Sadly this was their fiftieth anniversary week and neither one cared about it. A few weeks later, the nurse told me that they didn't expect her to make it through the weekend. I took a leave of absence from work and stayed there with her. Remarkably she started eating for me and became more alert. She helped me blow out her candles on her seventy-sixth birthday cake. She continued eating as much as she could and we enjoyed spending our days together. She lived another seven weeks after I took the leave of absence.

One morning when I went in to her room to get her up, I noticed her face was so smooth with no wrinkles. I knew that she was in the process of dying. I lay on the bed beside her and I stroked her hair from her forehead. She was smiling and I told her how much I loved her and how proud I was of her. I told her I knew she was tired and she could go be with my brother. I would be all right.

I called the nurse and she came out to the house right away. She agreed that it wouldn't be long and told me all the different signs of death. The nurse planned to stay there all day. We were able to get Mom out to the living room on the couch and make her comfortable. I called the preacher from our church and also my cousin. A few women from the church came and Mom lost

consciousness. As we kept her comfortable, she just kept hanging on, and in the evening all the visitors had left. Even the nurse went home, but I knew she would come when I needed her.

I kept Mom on the couch and pulled up a chair beside her so I could rest and keep my hands on her chest. I wanted to be awake when she passed. The night became morning and this day was pretty much the same. She was barely alive but her heart continued to beat. Even though she was unconscious she did something amazing.

All of a sudden, she started reaching up toward the ceiling and yelling, "Hoy! Hoy!" And she would smile and laugh. I sat back with my eyes about to pop out. Whoa! What was happening here? I realized she was calling out to my brother. She was calling my brother's name, Joey. She was looking up with her eyes open. She could see my brother in heaven. He must have been calling down to her. Then she relaxed again. She never did that again. I was so grateful that I was there to witness this beautiful conversation between them.

Her organs were beginning to shut down. The nurse came out to the house to check on her. She catherized her since her bladder was distended. Her blood was settling between her back ribs and her feet were becoming very dark, but her heart, which used to be so weak, kept beating. Another quiet night watch as I kept my hands on her chest, feeling her breathing, ever so shallow. I got the Bible and opened it up randomly and ran my finger down, stopping to read where it landed. Surprisingly my finger was pointing to Ecclesiastes 3: 1–4. "There is a time for everything, and a season for every activity

under heavens: a time to be born and a time to die, a time to plant and a time to uproot, a time to kill and a time to heal, a time to tear down and a time to build, a time to weep and a time to laugh, a time to mourn and a time to dance." Wow, yes God, I hear you. Thank you for comforting us through this time. I sat there holding the Bible in my lap after I had read it aloud to Mom. I gazed at Mom as she continued to breathe. I felt peace and I knew I was not alone. All was well.

Mom made it through another night. This was the fourth day. All her organs had shut down and her heart continued to beat. Later in the evening on July 21, 1996, she passed away. She weighed fifty pounds. I felt such a relief knowing she was finally at peace. She had struggled for so long, most of her life. I know my brother was there to welcome her home.

That following Christmas something amazing happened. The first time I heard "Silent Night" playing on the radio, a verse stood out loud and clear to me for the first time: "Mother and child/Sleep in heavenly peace." From that moment on, I cherished hearing this beautiful song.

Alzheimer's

> I will praise the Lord, who counsels me; even
> at night my heart instructs me. I keep my eyes
> always on the Lord. With him at my right hand,
> I will not be shaken.

Psalm 16: 7–8

Only two months after my Mom passed, I started
noticing Dad was doing really strange things. I
had been coming out every day to make sure he was
eating and his needs were being met. This particular day
I watched him water the silk flowers on the dining room
table. Earlier that week he was calling a realtor to give
them the house. He didn't want it anymore.

I made an appointment with his doctor and they felt
that it was probably Alzheimer's. Oh no. So I had to turn
my focus on this new situation to consider the options
for his future care. After talking it over with my husband,
we agreed to care for him at home, rather than a nursing
facility. We would have to remodel his house to make
it wheelchair accessible and big enough for the three
of us. I would need my space so I could rest and keep
my patience for I worked with folks with Alzheimer's. I

knew this was going to be a full-time job and I needed to properly prepare myself for this challenge.

First we had to find a reliable contractor. A friend recommended this man who had remodeled her home. We met with him with our ideas and he drew up the blueprints. We would be turning a one-story brick ranch into a two-story Cape Cod. There would be an in-law suite added for Dad. We would have to build a garage first so we could empty the house of all the stuff accumulated over the many years. My parents were from the Depression era and didn't throw anything away. I am sure you have known some people who have down the same. They kept all their old plastic butter bowls, old sheets, and towels. They always thought they could use it again someday. They had stuff stashed in all the back closets and attic. All this stuff would have to be removed from the house since we had to take the roof off to build the second story. Everything had to go. If it was salvageable, it would go to goodwill.

Once the footers were dug, we moved Dad to our house to keep him safe. I had talked to an adult day care and made arrangements for Dad to go there during the day while I worked. I knew he wouldn't want to go, so I told him it was his new job. They needed someone to talk to the people so they wouldn't be so lonely. He liked that and went for it.

I began to do all kinds of research on Alzheimer's. I read books and found ways to keep Dad busy doing manly stuff, like sorting nuts and bolts. Every case of this heart-breaking illness is different. They actually can't truly diagnose it except after death doing a brain autopsy. You

just have to do the best you can to help them keep their dignity. Find ways to help them continue living a happy and healthy life. I was afraid he would get lost. I went and signed him up with a company, which connected us with an identification bracelet he wore.

You also need to see an attorney to become their durable power of attorney to handle their legal, medical, and any other needs you may have forgotten about. I took care of all the legal matters and had everything in order.

Oh yeah, we didn't talk about the most important thing you need to do. Yes. Take the keys away so they cannot drive. Earlier when we were starting the construction, I took his keys away. He handed them right to me. Wow, that went much smoother than I expected. But Mister Sneaky had another set of keys. I came home from work one day and he mentioned he went and got gas for the lawnmower. What? How did you do that? I saw the look on his face like a little kid caught for being bad.

"Dad? Where are the car keys?" He suddenly reached down to cover his pants pocket. "Please give them to me."

"No way!"

So I actually had to wrestle with him till I had the keys. He was very angry, but I knew I had to take them. We also took his car away. When I told my dad's doctor at his next visit about taking away his keys, the doctor smiled and said, "My family and I thank you."

The house is now all remodeled. We sold my Tudor home and my cottage at the lake that I had inherited from my mom. We all moved in and are getting settled. Dad has his own area with a bedroom, a kitchenette, a

bathroom with walk-in shower, and small living room. I put all his familiar furniture in his place and he was safe. The kitchen had a small refrigerator and no stove. This way he could not burn himself or burn the house down. By now he had sundowners, which means he did not know night from day. I would lock his door at night. I had put a baby monitor in his room for his safety and the other in our bedroom. I could hear him when he cried out. He would sleep for a while and wake up thinking it was a new day. I went in many times during the night to reassure him. When we were home during the day, I let him roam around the whole house.

The worst thing we went through was that my dad needed to be circumcised. Yes, you heard me right. His urologist felt, because of cleanliness concern and possible swelling, it should be done before it could become an emergency situation. At this point, he didn't communicate well with words and wouldn't understand if I did tell him. Can you imagine? It was like taking a pet to get it neutered. Hand in hand we walked into the outpatient surgical area and sat down, waiting for them to call his name.

My poor dad, he was now eighty-three years of age and I had to act calm and take him back to the room when they called his name. After he came out of recovery, they let me go see him. He was crying and kept looking down at himself. He couldn't understand what had happened to him. It was a big hassle trying to keep the ice bag on him. About an hour later they sent us home with directions to put cream on his penis every few hours. Oh boy, he was applying everything he could find to his

penis—hand soap, hand cream, etc. Keeping his pants on was a real challenge. By now he wore adult diapers since he had lost urinary control. He hated wearing them. He would tear them off and flush them down the toilet. I would find those tiny absorbent beads all over the floor. I was forever tapping the back of his pants to see if they made a plastic sound. When he was wearing depends, they would make a crinkle sound when patted. Once I thought he had on his depends until I saw urine running down his pants. He had taken them off and was wearing a plastic grocery bag with his legs through the handles. You never knew what to expect next. You had to laugh because he was always doing some comical things.

Once I took him to a large department store to do some shopping. We were walking along and he spit on the new carpet. I wanted to crawl in a hole and hide. I was embarrassed as I cleaned it up. We continued to look for this special gift we were buying for his great grandson. As I was looking through some clothing, I turned around and Dad had walked over to the checkout counter and started urinating on it. Oh no. I grabbed Dad and was apologizing to the clerk for the mess as we hurried out of the store. The customers were gasping as I looked away. That was the last time I ever took him shopping.

I never brought this up before, but my husband was very helpful with my dad's care. I did not personally trust my husband and still lived every day in fear. I was always frightened he would explode again. So I walked on glass. I had always suspected he wanted my inheritance. He often left to go motorcycle riding with his buddies. If he wasn't out riding, he was golfing.

I kept busy with Dad's care. I had taken a family leave of absence to better care for my Dad. Dad needed a lot of care and attention. Dad's health started to fail. He stopped walking and refused to eat. I was so worried when he wouldn't eat that I took him to the hospital, and after they examined him, they said there was nothing they could do for him. I called my pastor and he came out for a visit. I told him how I was so worried, maybe we should have him tube fed. The pastor reassured me that I was doing the best for my Dad and I had to realize that he was in the final stages of Alzheimer's. I then took my pastor to the side and I discussed my real fears with him. I told them about the past police issues with my husband and how I was scared of him. I feared that when my Dad died and I was alone, my husband would become abusive again. I needed to tell someone, just in case something happened to me. I felt relieved as the pastor told me he understood and had actually known about the gun issue from one of the parishioners.

We had a hospital bed delivered to the house. I called hospice to arrange for their help with Dad's care. They were scheduled to start the next morning. It became apparent that Dad's health was deteriorating quickly. My husband recommended that this would be a good time to talk to him and say what I wanted to say. I went into his room and held his hand. He was awake and I think he could hear me. I told Dad that I loved him and that he worked hard for his family. He looked into my eyes but he did not speak. I reassured him some more that he could go and be with Mom. I knew how tired he was. He took another breath, and as I held his hand, he passed away.

He had lived four years after he was diagnosed with Alzheimer's. I called the doctor and told him Dad had passed. Then I called the police department. When someone dies without home health care or hospice, you need to have the police out. They have to make sure this was a natural death.

The police came, took pictures, and checked our identification—yes, they did. Guess what? My husband had an outstanding warrant for his arrest. If this had been the sheriff department, they would have taken him into custody. This was a small-town police department and they told him to take care of it soon. An ambulance came and took Dad's body to the hospital where they could declare him dead for the death certificate. I had to go to the hospital to release his body to the funeral home. Since Mom had home health care and I had made all her arrangements prior to her death, the home health nurse declared her time of death and the funeral home came and got her. It was so much easier.

We made the arrangements to have his calling hours at the church and Dad was buried beside Mom in the cemetery, a short distance from where Joey is buried. I felt proud of myself for being there for my Dad's care and keeping him comfortable and as happy as I could. Some people who knew my family for a long time told me that it was amazing that I stepped up to care for this man who had abused my mom and me. I told them it was not at all easy, but I was blessed that his attitude had changed with the Alzheimer's. He became loving and he did tell me how much he loved me. What a complete change over the years. He died peacefully. And I found the love from my Dad that I always craved.

911

The righteous cry out, and the Lord hears them; he delivers them from all their troubles. The Lord is close to the brokenhearted and saves those who are crushed in spirit.

Psalm 34: 17–18

After Dad passed away, I went back to work. This time I worked with the profound adults in a classroom setting. These adults are severely disabled and have many fragile health challenges. Besides their basic needs of being fed and changed, we encouraged them to do activities. Depending on their abilities, we helped them strengthen their muscles and stimulate their senses. I kept busy creating and designing activities for each individual's needs. There was lots of paperwork to document their progress and team meetings to decide their new goals.

These adults became my second family. And they grabbed my heart. Looking into their loving eyes and seeing their smiles was very rewarding. Now truthfully, they can be very stubborn and they have behavior problems. Most of the clients could not communicate other than a scream or moan. You have to try to find why they were upset. Maybe they had a headache or were ill or possibly another staff or client made them angry. It could be a multitude of things that could be upsetting them. We had to try to understand what they were trying to tell us. But I loved my job and I loved these people.

Now about my home life, well, my husband became more cold and distant. He quit his job and started a small heating and cooling business. If a buddy wanted to go riding or golfing, he would go. He worked if and when he wanted to. He started spending our money on new golf clubs and a used truck. Now he wanted to buy a new motorcycle. He wasn't making any money. I went to work every day and who did he think he was to think he could retire and play all day? He didn't have any pension or income. I put my foot down about a new motorcycle.

I had always been so careful not to upset him, but enough was enough. What was I going to do to get out of this mess? And stay alive? I contacted a lawyer and was told to have a secret bag packed if I had to leave quickly. So I just kept quiet and painted in my studio in my spare time. In the meantime he just became mean and nasty. He criticized everything I did and I felt so inadequate.

As I was leaving for an in-service for work one morning, he would not let me leave. He blocked my car, so I went into the house to distract him, and when he followed me in, I ran back out and got in my car and drove away. Whew! Scared and I was very nervous but I was safe. I knew he wouldn't know where I was going. The staff were scheduled to go to different locations

for their different certification requirements. When I arrived at my meeting place, I called my lawyer and scheduled to meet with her later.

When the training in-service was over and the staff were excused for lunch, I was walking out with some coworkers. I saw him in his truck in the parking lot. How on earth did he find me? A bunch of us were meeting at a fast-food restaurant down the street. I quickly ran to my car and got in and started to drive off. By then he was driving behind me and tried to run my car off the road. I just went a little faster as my heart beat harder. This was not good and I was scared to death. I did not have a cell phone. This was not going to end well. I did make it to the restaurant. I parked by a friend and I motioned to her to look at him. She stayed beside me as we went in together. He stayed out in the parking lot till he eventually drove away.

After lunch we got in our separate cars and left for the next location, one of our workshops. He wouldn't know I was there. Looking around to make sure he wasn't hiding, my friends walked in with me to our next class. A few hours later when this class ended, we went out to get in our cars when I saw his head duck down. Oh no. He was here. I went to go back inside when he drove up and grabbed my arm, pulling me toward his truck. I screamed and a male staff started coming to help me. He let go of my arm and I ran inside the workshop. I called the police and my lawyer. I waited by the door and I saw him take off down the road. I ran out and got in my car and drove off in the opposite direction and headed toward the lawyer's office. I made it there safe.

At the lawyer's, we made a police report and filed for a restraining order. She asked if there was somewhere I could go for a few days. I called my brother's widow and she let me hide there. I left the lawyer and I drove to her small town, we parked my car inside her garage.

This was the weekend and she made me feel comfortable as I hid away. I was concerned for my dogs at home and knew I couldn't do anything about it. I did not want anyone to know where I was. I did call my sons though so they would know I was safe. My sister-in-law was home recovering from surgery so I was able to drive her car to work. My coworkers would walk in and out with me from work. The management had a code to protect the staff if he should enter the worksite. I kept calling the police, but they were unable to serve him the protection order. He had been able to avoid the police for ten days until they were finally able to serve him.

I finally went home. I had contacted a security company and they installed a home security alarm that day. I could see him driving by the house. My house was way out in the country, far from the sheriff's department. The sheriff did drive by and check on me quite often though. I still was a basket case. In the meantime my husband, ugh, was calling everyone telling them I was a mental case and without my medication. He also emptied my house of my computer, family photographs, my Dad's army rifles. You name it, he took it. He had my address book and seriously called everyone in it.

In the meantime he would go to my church and take the bibles and lay them outside of my house while I was working. I would find notes on my car. The last straw

was in church one Sunday. I had been to the pastor a few weeks prior to talk about my situation. My family and I had been going to this church for forty years now. Many pastors had come and gone over the years and this one was fairly new. As I sat in the pew, the preacher was standing behind the pulpit and literally asked if everyone would pray for Sally and ——(his name). They were having problems in their marriage. Never in all the years that I went there did I ever hear a pastor mention names. Maybe asking us to pray for couples but never mentioned names. And doesn't a preacher honor the confidentiality when talking to a parishioner? I sat in that pew and melted. My church family was all I had left in town. Mr. Charmer had quite an influence on people. I know, he charmed me many times. He was good at it; in fact, he made his living from charming women and living off them. I was so devastated that I quietly got up and walked out as soon as the service was over. I never intended to ever come back.

His lawyer was really good. I believe he was much better than mine. But I was so thankful that I had kept all the receipts and documents, all organized in a folder. I just remembered a funny story I forgot to tell you. When he gave me my engagement ring, he had gotten it at a rental center. Yes, a rent-to-own engagement ring. I found the receipt. It was a real diamond though. Anyway back to the lawyers, with all my gathered receipts, I was able to prove that everything was in Dad's name. With all the house construction, it was all started in my Dad's name. He had no right to any of it.

The nice girl that I am, I did pack up everything that he had when he moved in, and I gave him his motorcycle and golf clubs. But his lawyer delayed the court case for months. I later found out through my insurance paperwork that he had back surgery while he was still covered under my insurance. After he recovered, the dissolution became final. He still played his games, my car was keyed, and he stole my lawnmower from the garage. I often came home and the garage door opener was disconnected.

Luckily he found another sweet innocent girl to charm and mooch off. Hopefully they are together a long time, happily ever after. I did my time. He has left me alone.

Stitch by Stitch

Trust in the Lord with all your heart and lean
not on your own understanding; in all your ways
submit to him, and he will make your paths
straight.

Proverbs 3: 5–6

B ill and I had worked together at a facility for
disabled adults. We worked at different workshops
but I would occasionally see him at classes or training
in-services to keep our certifications up to date. Bill was
a quiet guy who kept to himself. He was very handsome
with dark hair and was good working with his people. I
liked the way he showed his clients respect and I could
see how much they adored him. He worked with non-
ambulatory folks, people who had to use wheelchairs to
get around. He attended to their needs and supported
them while they performed their tasks. They packaged
items for businesses or folded business forms. There
were lots of jobs his people were able to do.

Since this was a workshop, we provide work for them
to do and they earn a paycheck. I often say we find the
abilities in people who were labeled disabled. When Bill

and I attended the training seminars, Bill would always tell us stories about his bicycle rides. He was in the bike club and they rode on long distance trips. I heard him say that he had logged over four thousand miles for that year. There were some groups of riders who went for out-of-state trips. It was very evident how much passion he had for bike-riding. I was very impressed although I had no desire to ride a bike. I didn't know much about his private life other than he was single and also worked an extra job besides his full-time job.

About the time my dissolution was final, Bill was transferred to the workshop where I was working. It was awesome since he was such a good team worker. I worked in the back of the workshop in a classroom and stayed to myself. Bill's area was out in the open area of the contract floor. After the clients left for the day, staff would get together in different rooms to discuss clients and do their paperwork. It was nice sharing time with my coworkers and I enjoyed time to laugh about life, and my friends were very supportive of the rough time I was going through.

Walking out of work one day, Bill approached me and said he and his parents were going out for dinner, and maybe I would like to join them just to get out. He knew I had the protection order and lived my life in fear. He said that he talked to his parents and they wanted me to come. I told him that would be nice and I would meet them there.

His Mom and Dad were very nice. Bill had already told them about my situation and they made me feel comfortable. His mom was so nice and it was great to

talk to another woman about my life. We had a great time and it was fun to be out and to laugh. A few weeks later his parents were going out again and they asked me to join them. This time some friends of the family had joined the group and they were so nice. It was so good just to have some new people in my life. They made me feel special. Bill's mom knew that it was risky and we never knew if we would run into my ex somewhere. His mom made me feel comfortable and told me to relax as they would protect me.

I was blessed to be invited to join them for the holidays. Bill and I were just friends and it was so good to have people to visit and spend time with. This was my only opportunity to spend time with people outside of work, and their support was so comforting.

This would be a great time to tell you more about Bill. Bill is a true miracle. Bill loved to run cross-country in high school and was very good at it. After graduation he went to Grove City College in Pennsylvania and continued to run cross-country. I understand that it was about this time in his life when he started having seizures. They were more of an aura, a trance state. He ignored these seizures and continued to run. He ran the Boston marathon as well as the Cleveland marathon. He didn't win but he ran a very good race.

He graduated from college and found a job out west in southern California managing a store. His seizures were coming on more frequently and stronger. One day he blacked out while driving and drove into a large department store. Luckily no one was hurt other than Bill. It was time for Bill to come home to Canton to

seek medical help. He also needed the support of his family. The seizures were very bad and continued to come on stronger and longer. He was diagnosed with epilepsy. What a terrible thing to happen to a young man. He could no longer drive or work. He was totally dependent on his family. The doctors tried many medications, different doses, different kinds, hoping to find what would work for Bill. It took a lot of trial and error to find the medication that would help. This took months and lots of waiting. He studied up on epilepsy and joined the epilepsy society. He eventually became president. It must have helped him a lot during those sad days to have other people to talk to, people who shared his same illness.

The medications helped to calm the seizures but did not totally take them away. Bill started doing counted cross-stitch embroidery to keep his sanity. He didn't do simple designs either. His pictures are so detailed, beautifully and neatly done. One of his pictures is the Lord's last supper, perfectly stitched with so many blends of beautiful colors, a gorgeous piece of artwork. I really like the United States Capitol building. It is completed with details of black and white. It is bordered with bright red tulips, absolutely stunning.

When I look at the framed pieces I can only imagine the heartache and frustration he was going through as he stitched them, one stitch at a time. These pictures are big, filled in completely with lots of stitches, lots of time dedicated to his artwork. While stitching each stitch, he attempted to maintain some balance in his life. To be a college graduate working at a great job on his own and

now being dependent on someone to drive him to his doctor's appointments. It took some time but he finally qualified for financial government assistance.

His seizures were getting worse. Bill's neurologist was looking into some new experimental surgeries that Bill might be a good candidate for. This surgery was very risky and would require opening his brain to remove the part of the brain that was causing the seizures. They would probe at different parts of his brain to try to determine where the damaged area was. Different parts of the brain control different organs and different body parts. The brain is the main control center of the body, like the computer. They would perform this surgery in Cleveland Clinic Hospital. They have such a great reputation with their research and up-to-date, trained doctors. This was a very scary life-threatening decision for Bill and his parents to make. Bill will tell you that at this point in his life, he wasn't really living anyway. What did he have to lose? This was in the year of 1984.

They prepared him for surgery. They shaved his head and gave him medicine to relax him. After being put to sleep, they cut his scalp and then removed a section of his skull to expose the brain. After probing around in his brain, they found the tissue that they felt was causing the seizures. Gratefully praising God, Bill came through the surgery fine. It would take some time after recovering to see if the surgery was successful.

Unfortunately his seizures soon came back and with a vengeance. It had to be so disappointing to lose the hope they had. Bill had to face the reality that he would be dependent on everyone for the rest of his life. Very

depressed, he started to work on his counted cross-stitch pictures again. He was having more grand mal seizures than ever before. He continued to work on his pictures between seizures. After a seizure his body is totally exhausted and he would have to sleep for hours. I am so impressed with the way he found contentment even though he didn't always feel like stitching. But I will tell you, these pictures were so perfectly stitched with so many colors of threads and tiny stitches. I know he only had time on his hands just surviving, but to all those minutes, hours, days, weeks, months, and years stitching day in and day out, he had dedicated so much time into making beautiful pictures. That is so amazing to me, during all those hopeless days to turn them into beautiful works of art, to take his ashes and turn them into framed pieces of lasting artwork.

I am excited to tell you that eight years later they tried the surgery again. This time they were successful. The neurosurgeon removed the damaged brain tissue that caused the seizures. Unfortunately part of the tissue they removed affects his memory. But that is such a small price to pay when you have a miraculous seizure-free life. This was the year 1992. This all happened before I ever met Bill. I have never seen Bill have a seizure.

After Bill recovered and started his new life, I can only imagine how enthusiastic and energized he became. I have a joke I often tell people. They removed part of the brain but replaced it with the Energizer or Eveready battery. I think he wants to make up for all the lost time. This man is the most determined man I ever met. Two years after the successful miraculous surgery, he was

hired at the workshop working with the disabled. I was hired the year after Bill was. We met at a training class.

Now back to where we left off before I shared about Bill's past life. It was great having a friend like Bill in my life. He was so supportive and understood my emotional breakdowns and the times I would fall apart. He knew how much I missed my sons and my grandson. I couldn't help but begin to fall in love with him. He was not only compassionate but very handsome. I could tell he was also smitten with me.

We took a drive over to Philadelphia so I could introduce him to my oldest son, Jason. And of course give my baby grandson some hugs. Bill had never married and didn't have any children. I was thrilled when Jason and Bill hit it off instantly. I had shared with Jason about all Bill had been through with his epilepsy and all that he had overcome. Jason was very impressed with Bill's cycling. We visited for a few days. I was always very sad when I had to say good-bye and head back to my home. I missed so much of Alex and watching him grow up. I really wished we lived closer. Eight-hour drive away is a long drive. But it is what it is. When Jason was in the navy as a corpsman, he met a pretty girl from Philly, and now you know why they live there. Bill and I both had good jobs in Ohio. We plan on staying here until Bill retires.

Prince William

The Lord God said, it is not good for man to be alone. I will make a helper suitable for him.

Genesis 2: 18

August 5, 2003, Bill has a friend in his bicycle club who is a commercial pilot for a large airline. He also owns his own little plane. Bill called me and he was so excited I could hardly understand him. His friend offered to take both of us up for a plane ride, would I like to go? Oh yes, I love to fly and have never been in a small four seat plane before.

What I hadn't known was Bill had other plans in his mind. He was planning to propose to me while we were flying above North Canton. While we were driving behind the Akron-Canton Airport, we kept looking for the hanger where his friend's plane was stored. We found Al's car parked by the hanger and we got out of the car. There was this sweet little plane. I was so thrilled to be able to have this opportunity. Bill helped Al push the plane from the hanger. Al gave the plane a good go-over, making sure everything was in good working order. We were ready to fly and very nervous. We literally crawled up on the wing so we could reach the door to climb in. I found my way to the backseat. Then Bill squeezed in beside me. His friend gave us each a pair of headphones to put on so we could communicate with each other. It was so interesting watching Al click on all the instrument gages and prepare for takeoff.

The plane's engine started and my enthusiasm was bubbling over as the plane started moving toward the runway. We were okay for takeoff and away we went. Soon we were off the ground and heading up toward the clouds. I had my nose pushed to the window pane because I wanted to see everything. I was like a little kid and couldn't get enough of the view below me. I recognized many places, water towers, baseball fields, and I was just enjoying this whole experience.

Bill interrupted me, and I turned around to see what he wanted. I was a little disturbed since I was watching the scenery below. I wanted to keep watching out the window. He reached for my hand. What was he doing? He started talking and I looked at him, what? He asked me, "Will you marry me?" What? And he began sliding this beautiful diamond ring on my finger. I don't know whose hand was shaking more, his or mine. I couldn't believe it! Yes, Bill! Yes! After kissing some ugly frogs (ugh), my prince had finally arrived, my Prince William. Bill was the nicest, kindest, cutest man in the world. I looked up and saw his pilot friend grinning with the biggest smile. Maybe Bill chose to propose to me up in the sky since he could push me out if I said no.

This was so romantic, to learn how much planning Bill had put into this proposal. It just shows what kind

of a sweet and caring man Bill is. Any woman would have loved to be his wife, but he asked me to marry him. The plane continued to fly, although I was flying high without a plane. I was overflowing with excitement. I did not know what to look at, the scenery below or my gorgeous ring. We landed soon after. As I crawled out of the plane, his pilot friend took a picture of me, one hand supporting myself against the door and the other hand was proudly showing off the ring. This was so unbelievable. My head was spinning of thoughts of everything that had just taken place. Bill was smiling and we were so much in love. This man I always admired was now going to be my husband.

We helped get the plane back in storage and thanked his friend for being such a huge part of our day. I thanked him for doing such a great job flying and getting us safe back on the ground. Overflowing with excitement we left and went to a restaurant to get something to eat. We shared with the other folks eating about our magnificent, romantic flight and showed off my new ring. Our waitress came back to our table carrying balloons as everyone cheered and clapped, congratulating us.

We started planning for our wedding. We chose to get married in our backyard with a small gathering of our friends. I always liked the numbers 3 and 8 and if we hurried with the plans, we could get married on 8-30-03, which was three weeks away. We arranged for a justice of the peace to marry us. Bill made a beautiful arbor and he painted it white. The arbor would be such a romantic place to repeat the vows of our love. I decorated the arbor with burgundy and pink silk roses and I added ivy

and white bows with long trailing streamers. The potted mums were in season so I placed some burgundy plants by the base of the arbor.

I purchased a beautiful long simple bridal gown. Bill was fitted with a new suit. We asked Bill's sister to sing and play her guitar. I asked his mom to read some special scriptures. I made my bouquet out of fresh roses and baby's breath.

Soon the guests were arriving including Jason and his family. The weather that day was perfect. I planned to dress upstairs. It was time to start. I could hear everyone gathering downstairs. The music started and I slowly walked down the stairs where my handsome prince was waiting for me at the bottom of the stairs. Bill and I walked outside hand in hand to the waiting justice of the peace under the arbor. We shared our vows. The scriptures were read and Bill's sister, Kathleen, played the guitar as she sang some special songs. We were now husband and wife. We all left for a restaurant to enjoy our wedding reception with our guests. The cake was decorated with pink and burgundy flowers. It all looked so lovely. After we shared some toasts, Bill and I cut the cake. We all enjoyed good food and good times with our family and friends. They all blessed our new life together. My life was now so awesome, so unbelievably peaceful. We left for our honeymoon in Roscoe Village for a few days.

As we settled down into our newly married life, I wanted to share some of Bill's passions. I decided I would try riding my bicycle. I had this bike for many years. It needed tuning up and we had taken it to a bike shop to have it oiled and polished. Since Bill is very experienced he adjusted my seat for the appropriate leg extension for my legs. I was ready to ride. Remember this old grandma hadn't ridden a bike for years and was not used to the higher seat. While we were out on our first ride together, I fell and skinned my knee really bad. Since we were away from home, Bill tied his hankie around my knee till we could get home and bandage it properly.

A few weeks after my knee healed, I decided to get back on the bike and ride again. I went by myself and rode around our neighborhood and was actually doing quite well. I was getting used to the gears and felt comfortable. On the way home, I fell again. This time I heard a pop. Oh no. I got up and struggled with the bike, pushing it back home. I went into the house and grabbed the ice bag and flopped on the couch. I thought I broke my knee cap.

Bill came home and saw his poor wife injured with an ice bag on her knee. What did you do? he asked. When I shared about falling off the bike again, he just shook his head while looking at his uncoordinated wife. We went to the emergency room and they examined me. Story of my life, my ACL was torn and needed to be reconstructed.

I found a great orthopedic surgeon. I had my ACL surgically reconstructed. This is normally a football injury and I just couldn't believe this had happened from riding my bike. After I recovered from the surgery, I had to spend a lot of hours in physical therapy regaining the strength in my leg muscles. I am an artist and it is not worth the risk of breaking my arms or wrists. Yes, I gave up bike riding. I now kiss Bill good-bye and wave to him as he leaves to join the other bikers. I enjoy my quiet time painting in my studio doing my passion while Bill is enjoying his. Life is good.

The Awakening

> I sought the Lord, and he answered me: he
> delivered me from all my fears. Those who look
> to him are radiant; their faces are never covered
> with shame.
>
> Psalm 34: 4–5

We are happily married. We continued working together at the same workshop. Bill had his work area and I had mine. Everything was going so smoothly. I could now relax and take some time to learn who I really was. I was finally with someone who supported me for who I was. But who was I? I was never good at being me. Everyone made me feel I wasn't good enough, I never had any value. I had just learned to survive and mold myself into what people wanted me to be. I felt like the person who had multiple personalities, always becoming what people thought I should be. I was definitely a people pleaser. I lived to make everyone else happy. It never mattered how I felt. I had learned to dump my feelings inside, dumped down into deep crevices. It didn't hurt if I wouldn't let myself feel. And all this baggage, this stuff shoved inside was extending and dragging behind me. I had brought all my stuff with me into my new life. No, I didn't unpack my baggage. I just continued to drag it around. Wherever I went, it followed me.

My adorable husband—my loving, compassionate, caring man—started getting some of the trash dumped on him. Not on purpose, of course not, but emotions would bubble up and seep its ugly head into our life. All Bill had to do was say something that might touch a painful spot from my past. I found out that the more I learned to trust people, my deep dark baggage felt safe to crawl out. I am sure it must have been very crowded in the dark, dreary spaces of my heart as it yearned to escape. These outbursts of emotions would cause Bill pain. He couldn't understand. He never wanted to hurt me, but these dark memories would rise to the surface and all I wanted to do was run and hide.

Bill is Catholic, and since I had left my church, I didn't have a church to call my own. I knew I needed counseling. I was sinking into depression and hopelessness. I asked the secretary at Bill's church who the priest recommended for counseling. She would ask him and get back to me. He had recommended a counseling group in Akron. Akron? Why so far away? I found out it was actually south Akron so it was close enough. She recommended I get on their website and check them out.

Anxiously I got on their website and they had all the pictures of the therapists and their specialties. I scanned through each one and read their information. Two ladies caught my attention right away. I went back and forth

between their photos to see which one would catch my heart. It was Amy. I called the office and made an appointment for the first available time she had open.

I can't explain it but I felt hope that she was the one who could help me. I had to wait several weeks until my appointment and the day had finally arrived. On the drive up there, I was contemplating what I would say. Walking into the waiting room, I nervously looked around. The room was full of people of all ages. I reported in at the window and took a seat while waiting for my special Amy to appear. I saw her walking toward me and I felt a connection right away. I loved her spunky, cute outfit with her long, wavy red hair. Smiling, she reached out to shake my hand and asked me to follow her downstairs to her office.

I wanted a Christian therapist and was relieved when we walked into her office. It had such a warm personality and there were signs of God throughout the room. She had a sandlewood scented candle burning and I noticed several whimsical pieces of artwork hanging around the room. She motioned for me to sit in a large comfortable chair as she sat down across from me.

"Tell me about yourself, Sally."

That was all it took when the tears started flowing out. She handed me some tissues and said it was okay to cry.

"Where do I begin?" as I asked through my tears.

My life is so complex and I was a mess. I told her about my molestation as a child. She would just sigh and let me know she truly understood and felt the pain.

She could see the tightness with my breathing and tight fisted hands.

"Sally, let us stop a moment so you can take some deep breaths. I want you to breathe from deep inside, where your diaphragm is."

"Breathe in and breathe out, taking deep, deep breaths."

She showed me how to take deep breaths and let myself relax. For years I always thought I had some sort of goiter in the front of my neck from the large lump of tightness that often appeared. She explained how that was the stress and anxiety. She recommended that I start journaling my feelings down on paper every day. To find a plain notebook, nothing pretty for this was just to release my emotions. I was to write several pages a day. Before I knew it, our session was up and I made several appointments for the next month. I walked out of the building with swollen red eyes but with great relief knowing God had brought me help. Someone truly understood my pain.

I went home to share with Bill about my new therapist and how I felt so comfortable with her. I found a notebook and was excited to start to journal. I knew it would take a long time and a lot of sessions, but I was finally getting the help I had needed all my life. I have been to therapy before, for over twenty years in the past, but they were only temporary fixes to survive in the life I was living at the time. The therapy was a simple Band-Aid trying to mend a large oozing sore until the next abusive time when it was ripped open again. This was going to be different. My husband was a soft-spoken, caring man who loved me for who I was. I was learning

to trust him, although I wasn't able to trust myself, let alone anyone else.

Even though the sessions were often painful, I couldn't wait till my next appointment. Amy had such a warm smile and I knew she really wanted to help me resolve these demons. I felt so relaxed with her. She helped bring up the deep anger from my soul and help me release it. I found that these years and years of buried stuff would take many layers upon layers to uncover it. It was like a salad buffet where you take a plate, another one pops up, these were my issues. We would heal one and another one would crawl out. I was drowning in so much frustration and bitterness. Bill was so supportive and loving as I worked through all these painful emotions. I know it had to be very hard for my sweet husband.

Although I continued working for the workshop, I had changed jobs. I was working with individuals outside the workshop. We did janitorial work cleaning businesses. I would take a van of eight people and supervise them as we cleaned offices and different companies that contracted our services. They vacuumed, washed floors, and scrubbed bathrooms. They emptied the trash and any other cleaning required at a worksite.

The next few months as I continued therapy, my desire to paint came back. I applied for the large craft shows and was thrilled when they accepted me. So with Bill's blessing, I quit my job and started my own painting business. I named it Cottage Garden Creations and started painting everything I could. I painted wood plaques, slates, and even furniture. I set up a studio in

one of the upstairs bedrooms and this became my new home. These shows were scheduled in the fall so I had a few months to build up stock. I would need lots of artwork ready to sell. So I painted and loved it. I would sit at my painting table and listen to music and create artwork. I always felt God gave me a gift and I was thrilled to be using it.

Vows in the Church

Open for me the gates of the righteous; I will enter and give thanks to the Lord. This is the gate of the Lord through which righteous may enter. I will give you thanks, for you answered me; you have become my salvation.

Psalm 118: 19–21

Bill and I would have preferred to have said our first wedding vows in the church. But what church? Since I had left my childhood church during the divorce from the second marriage, I had no church to call my own. Bill was born Catholic. My Dad was Catholic but my Mom wasn't. My parents were married by a Catholic priest. To settle the choice of which church they would attend, they decided to go to the nearest church to where they would live. It happened to be a Methodist church. So I was raised a Methodist until they moved again. This time they moved close to the United Methodist Church. My family had gone to this church for forty years or so. I had my Dad's calling hours and funeral there. So walking away from this place was hard and very lonely for me. My Dad's sister and relatives who reside in a small town an hour south of here are all Catholic. I felt God calling me to the Catholic Church.

I signed up for the RCIA classes but had trouble attaining my annulment. This is a requirement of the Catholic Church to have any previous marriages annulled. My fellow classmates in the RCIA class went on and were confirmed Catholic. Not me. I was encouraged to attend another year of RCIA classes until the annulment would come through. I didn't have any witnesses left from my past who could verify my troubled marriages.

At this time Pope John Paul was becoming ill and the priest from the church we went to left to study in Rome. I laughed since the pope was Polish like me, and surely he would want me to be a member of the Catholic Church. I felt sad since my priest wasn't in town to help me. Unfortunately the pope died, and after our priest came back from Italy, he became ill and died. The door was not opening for me. I was so frustrated and I gave up trying. My Dad's sister passed away that summer and there was a memorial service at the church down south. As I sat there among my cousins, I knew the Catholic prayers by heart. I studied them at all the RCIA classes. I felt that I was one of them but just could not become Catholic.

Late in the fall I was shopping at our neighborhood grocery store when I encountered this cute little lady about forty something years of age. She was bent down grabbing all these cans of tomato sauce. They were on sale and she was determined to buy them all. Usually I wouldn't say anything, but this time I did. "Boy, you sure

are limber, getting up and down so easily." She said she worked out at a ladies gym. She also commented how a personal trainer had helped her strengthen her back muscles, helping to eliminate her back pain. She reached out her hand and said my name was Jo. I smiled and laughed while I shook her hand. I told her I should have known. Everyone who mattered in my family was named Joe. My dad was Joe, my brother was Joey, all my cousin's names have Joe in them—Mary Jo, Joanne, Josephine, Elizabeth Jo just to name a few. She told me she was buying all this sauce for her church, a Catholic Church. After she told me where her church was, she asked me to visit her church sometime. I shared my efforts to join the church. She asked if I would like to go out for lunch sometime. I would love to. We exchanged phone numbers and planned on doing lunch the next day.

I went home and couldn't help but laugh when I told Bill I was having lunch with someone I met at the grocery store. He asked who they were, and when I said Jo, he gave me a very puzzled look. "No, Bill, she is a girl," I had to assure him.

The next day Jo and I met at this healthy restaurant that serves awesome fresh sandwiches. She shared that she only eats healthy food, and by her cute slim shape, she could have been a model. I told her all about my boys and she told me about her son. She told me about the wonderful priest and her church. This church is an Italian Catholic Church and that they make and sell pizzas one Sunday a month. In fact this coming Sunday was pizza day. So she talked me into helping with the making of the pizzas.

She picked me up at five in the morning the following Sunday. This was really crazy for me but she was so much fun to be around that I wanted to be there. She introduced me to Father Tom. I felt his warmth instantly. He had such a comforting nature about him. Jo told him that I needed to talk with him when he had time. We set up an appointment that following week.

I came in with all my paperwork from the RCIA classes from the other church. I also brought in copies of all the paperwork that had been sent to the diocese trying to obtain the annulment. He asked me to start going to the RCIA classes at this parish just to get to know more of the other parishioners. I would like that. So I started going to the weekly evening classes and the months went by. Nothing happened for me except I learned a lot more. It was sad sitting there watching the class going through their first communion without me. Father Tom reassured me that it would happen, just not yet.

Bill and I continued to go to mass at this church even though I could not partake in the sacrament. After three years of trying, the annulment was finally granted. Father Tom received the paperwork. He called me and asked if Bill and I were ready to do our wedding vows in the church. Of course I was. But my first question was, don't I need to become Catholic first? He laughed and said you will receive your first communion all at the same time. He thought it would be fun to have us say our vows after a four o'clock Saturday mass. He checked his schedule and asked about May 26, 2007. I was astonished since that was my birthday. I told Father Tom and he was as excited as I was.

Seven months after I met Jo, I was here at my new church taking my first communion. Bill's family was there and I had Jo stand up for me. Bill and I exchanged our wedding vows, and it couldn't have been more perfect. The people here at the afternoon mass were clapping and cheering as Father Tom finished the wedding ceremony. I was reborn on my birthday and was now of the Catholic faith along with my husband.

We have three grandchildren. Alex is our first-born grandson and is ten years old. Allison, our only granddaughter whom we call her Allie, is eight years old. Matthew is our youngest grandson and is three years old. They live close to Philadelphia, Pennsylvania, with my oldest son and his wife, Lisa. It breaks my heart to live an eight-hour drive away from them. I miss so much of their lives. When I do get a chance to visit them, I cherish being their grandma and love to spoil them. Every now and then I send them clippings of houses for sale in my neighborhood, tempting them to move close to me. So far it hasn't worked, but I am still hoping.

My youngest son, Chris, is getting married August 2013. He is marrying the girl of his dreams, Jeannine. They live in Alaska. Bill and I are hoping to attend their wedding. It will be our tenth wedding anniversary that month. What a great time to go to Alaska and celebrate.

Most of my friends are blessed to have their families close to home. It breaks my heart to live so far away from my sons. I remind myself that I am very blessed that they are healthy and happy. They love their homes and their jobs. I am extremely blessed that my sons have found women who love them and support them for who

they are. They live very enjoyable lives. What more could a mom want than to know she raised fine sons who are living their best life. I am very proud of my grown sons.

Last summer was the twentieth anniversary of Chris's miraculous recovery from his car accident. The boys thought it would be awesome to honor the fire department that rescued Chris that horrific night. Jason has a business that makes emergency rescue equipment. So the boys chose the equipment they felt would be of best use for the emergency squad. The equipment was made and personalized with our family name in honor of rescuing Chris. We scheduled a time that would work for the fire station for us to come and visit.

Chris flew in from Alaska and Jason drove over from Philadelphia with his family. The local newspaper was there and they wrote an article and took pictures of Chris donating the equipment. I was proud to present the fire captain with a plaque in honor of saving my son's life. The fire station captain and firemen were very appreciative of the new equipment. Jerome's mother was there along with her sister. It was a wonderful and emotional celebration.

This was the first time both my sons were home together in over eight years. Just knowing my sons and their families were all sleeping under my roof was heaven on earth. It was so awesome spending time with both my boys again. I will always cherish that memory.

Bill and I do share a passion together. We love dogs. We especially love Cavalier King Charles Spaniels. Our first one we brought home is named Abbey. She is a Blenheim, which means she is red and white colored. Our

second four-legged child is Rusty. He is tri-colored. Our third one is named Rudy. He is ruby colored. And last, and she will be the last, is Rosie. She is the youngest at six months and is black and tan. Yes, there are four kinds and we have all four. They all have different personalities and we cherish them all. Since Bill has never had any children, these are his kids. Bill will often come home from work and say, "Don't we have the greatest family?" They bring so much joy into our lives and it helps me from missing my grandchildren so much. I can cuddle with them since they are a medium-sized breed, and yes, they do live on our furniture. Maybe I should say they allow us to use their furniture. Bill built a wood dog-eared fence to enclose our backyard. The fence sure makes life easier when you have four dogs. They love the freedom of running and chasing the squirrels.

The Vessel

Yet you, Lord are our Father. We are the clay, you
are the potter; we are all the work of your hand.

Isaiah 64: 8

Bill and I were happy living our life together. Bill was
always looking for property to invest in as rentals
or to fix it up and sell. Bill has several rental properties,
which he owns and manages himself. And he has the
best cleaning lady. Of course that would be me. I clean
and help to prepare the places to be rented again after
someone moves out. I actually love cleaning them
and putting love back into them. I like to think that
we are home providers rather than landlords. And yes,
Bill is still working his full-time job at the workshop.
Remember this is Prince William with the Eveready
battery charged and energized.

We were driving around looking at property
foreclosures. Pulling out of a driveway of a house on our
list, my eyes caught this house across the street. Wow!
Look at that place! I loved the charm and I was curious.
We slowed down, and surprise, there was a For Sale sign
in the yard. We were not planning on buying a home

to move in, just checking out investment opportunities. Bill took down the information. We were both excited to find that this place was also a foreclosure, bank owned.

The next morning we called our realtor and she made an appointment for us to see it that afternoon. We met her there and I was like a kid in a candy shop running from room to room to see what treasures this place held. It had it all. This was a colonial two-story with an attached two-car garage and a gazebo sitting in the side yard. Inside I found two fireplaces, four bedrooms, and two and half baths. One particular bedroom upstairs would be perfect for my art studio. It has sliding glass doors that lead to a second-story balcony. This balcony looks out over the fenced-in backyard, which is bordered by a wooded area. As a bird lover I was elated. This place was so inspirationally perfect. I ran downstairs to share my good news.

That is when the realtor told us there were already three bids on the house, which were being turned in Monday, which was tomorrow since that day was Sunday. The bank would be making their decision. Luckily since we had been purchasing property for a while, we had the pre-approved loan paperwork. Bill really liked the house and property and it was in great shape. So we got busy talking with the realtor about a good offer for the bank. What were the other bids? I wanted this place and we had to come up with a good amount. We decided on a strong offer, which we added eight dollars and thirty cents to. Yes, that is our wedding date. We went home and would have to patiently wait till we heard from the bank the next afternoon.

The phone rang on Monday and my realtor told me to start packing. The bank had approved our bid. Yes! I called Bill at work and we were both so excited. A month later, after all the papers were signed, we moved into our new home. I set up my studio in the perfect room with a view. I had painted the walls a pale fresh yellow, which is an inspiring color. I love to spend my time up there. My creative juices flow freely and I paint all day.

At my next therapy session, Amy was delighted to hear how our new home was coming together. Each appointment I was releasing more and more darkness and anger. As the darkness came to the surface, I always felt the pain. I had to relive those terrible times. As they were set free, it left room for me to put good feelings and love inside. I was beginning to understand I was a good person. As it took many years to bury that baggage, it would take a long time to dig it up and release it.

I was very busy painting and preparing for these craft shows. When I wasn't in the studio, I was working on making our house a home. Jason called and wanted to know if I could paint on wine bottles. He had found several cases which were being thrown away. I wasn't sure and I hesitated, but said yes, I would take them. I was sure I can design something. The next week Jason packed up those empty cases and his family and drove to Ohio for a long overdue visit. We were excited to show them our new home. And it was so good catching up on each other's lives. I cherish every opportunity when I can love my grandchildren up close and in person. Before long they were packing up and heading home.

After I tearfully waved good-bye watching their car drive away, I went back to the studio to design. The

ideas started flowing. Since my art business is Cottage Garden Creations, I would design a cottage around an empty wine bottle. Wow! Then I decided I would give the bottle several coats of paint to give the bottle texture like pottery. Another idea came and I asked Bill to drill a hole in the back of the bottle. I wanted to have lights shine through the windows of the cottage. I would mask out space for the windows so they would be clear. After many tries, Bill successfully had a perfect round hole drilled.

So now the fun begins. I had fun painting the details around the quaint windows, adding window boxes and rose vines growing up around the outside of the cottage. I painted an old wood door framed with rustic stones. I turned this bottle into a quaint English cottage, and with the added lights, it looked like someone was home. I also designed an Italian villa with grape vines growing up the walls. I gave the outside an old stucco appearance. They are so cool. It was amazing to take an old, discarded wine bottle and make it into something so charming and beautiful using paint. I only had another month before the craft shows began. I got real busy and painted dozens of these cottages, each were unique and different since they were all painted by hand.

As I was painting one day, I could hear God speaking to me. He was asking me if I knew why I was painting these bottles. Well? Amazed with his question, I was not sure but I loved doing it. He then spoke again.

"You are painting vessels."

"Vessels?"

"Yes, as I created you out of clay and made you my vessel, you are making vessels using the gift I gave you, your creativity. As I pour my love into you, the vessel, you then pour it onto someone else."

I love the opportunity to share with my customers this story. As the light shines through my painted vessels, I pray the light of God shines through me unto them. Hopefully I can pass along hope and encouragement to others I meet along my journey.

> You, Lord, keep my lamp burning; as God turns
> my darkness into light.
>
> Psalm 18: 28

This was a major turning point in my life. As I healed my anger with the help of Amy, I began feeling God tugging at my heart. I became more open toward God and listened for him to guide me.

We did the craft shows and they were successful. Bill is my financial manager. He would write up my sales and package up the purchases. This would free me to demonstrate and personalize my artwork. The people loved the cottages and we sold out at each show. This kept me very busy painting and preparing for the next show and each show after that.

This was our life for several years. Bill and I loved meeting the folks at the shows and it was fun painting and selling my artwork. In the off season, I helped Bill with the rentals. We are a good team. I continued going to my monthly therapy sessions and was making tremendous progress in my healing. I was learning more about myself, my limits, and was enjoying the person I was. I learned I could trust and allowed more people into my life. I was tearing down the wall I hid behind. I was learning to actually feel and have emotions of happiness.

What I want you as the reader to learn is to stop trying to swim upstream. God has a plan and purpose for each one of us. It is much easier to go with his flow. My life was actually all about survival in the past. As I let go of some stuff, I learned that there was a much easier way of life, one with less struggle.

Yankee Peddler Festival is a primitive outdoor craft show. When I was a young girl, I always loved going here. The finest crafts people demonstrate their talents and sell their artwork. The craftsman dressed in primitive attire and everything is constructed the old-fashioned way. No plastic or modern-day objects are used. What an honor when I was accepted to display and sell my artwork at their craft show.

They started a new section called Yankee Today. This allows the craftsman to use a little more modern supplies in the making of their artwork. Therefore, I could use electric lights in my bottles. They encourage the crafts people to create a piece of artwork made specifically for Yankee Peddler and Yankee Today. The artwork would then be judged in different categories, like most educational display, best craftsmanship, etc. I felt inspired to create a tall lighted bottle with the Marblehead Lighthouse on it. This was a two-foot tall blue wine bottle and I sculpted the lighthouse out of clay. I added clay for the rocks and the waves. I painted the lighthouse and the background of the wine bottle. I was very proud of this bottle. The Yankee Peddler judges must have liked it also since my piece won first place. And it came with a $250 award check.

We had been doing craft shows for four years now and we were setting up for one of the last shows of the season. I was struggling to carry boxes of supplies up the hill to our booth. I was panting and out of breath. This was not normal and I became concerned. I told Bill that I was extremely tired so I sat down while he continued to unload the supplies. We had a successful show, and by now, most of our customers were regulars and had a collection of my artwork. I would design a different lighted cottage for each season.

After the show, I made an appointment with my doctor. I was scared that my lungs were damaged by the spray finish I used on the bottles. They scheduled an appointment with a pulmonologist. My lungs were good. What could it be? They did some blood work and found the problem. I was anemic, and my iron was very low. I went to my gastroenterologist for an endoscope and colonoscopy. They found that I was bleeding internally from a tear in my hiatel hernia. They prescribed a stronger heartburn medication that would allow the tear to heal naturally.

At the last craft show I bought a chrysalis. This is the cocoon where a monarch butterfly comes from. I was excited to watch this transformation. The caterpillar had already turned into the chrysalis, and now after some time of growing, the butterfly would emerge. They have the chrysalis attached to the inside of a box with a screen covering the hole. This way you can watch and see the changes. When the craft show was over, I was thrilled that the shows were over since I was so tired but very anxious to be able to watch this amazing transformation.

Be Still and Know
That I Am God

Have mercy on me, O God, according to your unfailing love; according to your great compassion. Blot out my transgressions. Wash away all my iniquity and cleanse me from all sin.

Psalm 51: 1–2

Recovering from the anemia, I was thankful that the craft season had ended. I took it easy. I had put my little box with the monarch chrysalis on the kitchen counter so I could watch it closely. I read up on it and learned that the green-colored shell would darken as the butterfly developed. When the shell started to become clear, you could actually see the orange and black wings curled up inside. It was so amazing to watch this transformation.

It took several weeks of daily observing, anxiously waiting for my butterfly to emerge. Then one day it happened. Wow! He crawled out of the shell and was hanging upside down. He would pump his wings tightly together, which would expel this brown liquid, basically leftover stuff from the caterpillar. They pump their wings to help strengthen their body, preparing it to fly. I was so thankful for this opportunity to see this miraculous transformation. This experience has forever changed my life. I became obsessed with butterflies.

After a few days, I opened up the box and let the butterfly rest on my fingers. Just to spend some time together. I watched it step off my hand and onto a butterfly bush bloom. I was in such awe watching nature up so close. The butterfly took its first sip from the flower petal. Then after an hour it took its first flight and flew freely away.

I studied up on anemia. I wanted to learn all I could about what was happening to me, what I could do to assist my recovery. I found out that iron supplies the organs with oxygen, which then fuels them. Since I had little iron, I had no energy. It takes the body an average of three months to rebuild the hemoglobin in the blood. Besides the heavy dosage of iron pills I was taking daily, I would have to take it easy and rest for the next several months. So hey, I will just paint in the studio while I rest. Wrong. I also had lost all my desire and passion to paint. What was happening to me?

When we were fixing up this home, there was an extra living room besides the family room. Our other home had a sunroom and this one did not. So I took the sunroom furniture and arranged it in this room. Bill had painted the walls this marvelous grayish green. I painted my other furniture a cream color to match the sunroom furniture. I also painted my mom's antique desk along with an antique glass front cabinet. I found some old chairs at a garage sale and had fun decorating them to

coordinate. I put my Thomas Kincaid framed print above the mantle of the fireplace. This room has all kinds of pink roses and floral decorations throughout. It became my meditation room. I feel so peaceful in this sanctuary of mine. I call it my Son Room, where the Son Rose.

After finding out I was anemic, I spent a lot of days in my Son Room. I had my favorite comfy chair along with my favorite footstool positioned where I could watch the bird feeder through the window. I sat here for hours upon hours praying and meditating. I spent a lot of time talking to God and listening for his whispers. It didn't take long before I realized that I was in the midst of my own transformation. I was in fact in the chrysalis stage.

Be still and know that I am God.

Psalm 46: 10

At my next session Amy and I talked how this was a special time for God and me. He was doing something very special in my life. I was to rest and prepare for what he had planned. During this time, I truly was still enough and patient to hear him. And since he removed my passion to paint, he evidently wanted all of my attention, no distractions. What happened next was so amazing. Every day I would just sit in my Son Room for hours upon hours. I just let the thoughts come to my brain. Many times he brought to mind about people who I needed to forgive and also where I needed to find forgiveness. I would cry, actually wail out loud for hours, weeping and setting some deep pain free.

I was that frumpy caterpillar struggling with all that baggage. I was dragging all my stuff behind. God was

transforming me, showing me how to remove the stuff. So hour by hour, day by day, I prayed and forgave all the things, the people who had hurt me. It was such a freeing time. I felt better each day. I still would have bouts of anger. I was after all still human flesh, but it became easier. Life became easier. I was becoming stronger, more confident in who I was. I loved myself, and the more I learned that I loved myself, I was free to love Bill more. I was grateful to have this time alone with God during the day while Bill was at work. I could cry out as loud as I needed. I didn't have to keep the pain in anymore.

I found out as I released the pain and felt more peace, the more feelings I could feel—good, happy feelings. I used to numb all my feelings, the bad and the good, everything and everyone seemed to cause pain. I found out if you didn't let yourself any feel emotions then nothing would hurt. When you hurt so bad and depression takes over your life, it is all about survival just to make it through each day. The last thing you care about is happiness. That is not even in your vocabulary. You especially don't want to see other people happy either. I was so full of stinking thinking and it took over all of my thoughts. You are so miserable that you want everyone else to be miserable too. So this time made sense to me. God was making me sit still, quiet enough to hear him. I had no choice. He removed all my energy, my desire to paint, I was all his. I wasn't as frustrated and I began to enjoy this quiet time.

As the months went by, I became stronger and was recovering from the anemia. Bill was extremely thrilled

with my transformation. It had to be so hard for him to see me so angry before. He couldn't understand why I was angry and what had he done. He was so patient and tried so hard to comfort me during all these emotional outbursts. Maybe his epileptic brain surgery and having some of the memory loss probably helped him cope with this situation. I haven't talked much about his forgetfulness, but it does have some bonuses. When you get to know Bill, you will find that he loves shirts with pockets. He always carries his notes to remind him of things he needs to do.

My friend had gotten a job with a small workshop and asked if I wanted to apply for the substitute position. They made all kinds of crafts there. It would give me a chance to get out with people and I could still recover when I wasn't scheduled. I prayed about this and the door opened and I was hired.

The first day they had me train in a classroom. I didn't know these disabled people yet. I must tell you, I wasn't sure this was for me. These twelve adults had severe challenges, blind, deaf, and quite noisy. I had become used to my quiet time in the studio and especially the last few months of quiet daily meditation. These people were screaming, yelling, and I looked up to God and asked, "Are you sure this is your plan for my life?" It was a long day and I left very tried and definitely confused whether this was for me.

The next day was much nicer since I worked with the higher functioning adults and we could communicate. Assisting with their needs was much easier and quieter. On the third day I was excited since I was working in

the high-production area. There was a girl who I had worked with in the past when I worked in the ceramic department of another workshop. Her name is Tammy. I was thrilled to be with her again. She loved to paint. Tammy had spina bifida and couldn't talk or hear. She used a wheelchair. We had our own sign language and could communicate. So for the next year I loved every opportunity when I could work with her. She was always happy to see me. She would squeal with this happy sound and smile from ear to ear. This workshop made their income from selling the crafts that the folks made. Tammy was happily painting and selling her artwork in the gift shop. She was gifted and a very talented artist.

The next few months went fast. I still had no desire to do my own artwork and was very contented working at the workshop. Tammy became ill and we soon realized her only kidney was failing. She was admitted to the hospital. We were told to come up that evening to say our good-bye. I went in to see her. She was unconscious in the intensive care unit. The family had requested for the hospital not to do any major attempts to save her and to allow her to die peacefully. I held her hand and brushed her hair from her forehead. I loved Tammy so much. I have had to say good-bye to so many people and this was going to be hard. As I held her warm hand, I told her to be strong and that I loved her. I bent down and kissed her forehead and tearfully left the room.

The next morning at work, we were informed that Tammy had passed during the night. My coworker and I started crying. My heart was so broken. Tammy was fifty-one years old. It was a sad day as we shared with

the other clients that Tammy had died. They had loved her too. I tried to do my job that day, but actually I was a basket case. Not much was accomplished.

Tammy loved the Cleveland Browns Football team so the family requested that we would wear Cleveland Brown's attire to her calling hours. I came to say good-bye wearing a Brown's scarf around my neck. Tammy looked so peaceful and she was out of her wheelchair. I felt God telling me that Tammy was now flying free in her butterfly form. She was no longer a frumpy grounded caterpillar and she was transformed and healed totally. She was released of all her stuff, leaving her wheelchair behind. She could now hear and talk as well as run through heaven's gates toward her savior. I felt so much peace.

Fly Free

> Give thanks to the Lord, for he is good; his love endures forever. Let the redeemed of the Lord tell their story – those he redeemed from the hand of the foe.
>
> Psalm 107: 1–2

The afternoon that Tammy passed, I shared my story with a friend about how God reassured me that Tammy was transformed from the frumpy grounded wheelchair caterpillar and was flying free as a beautiful butterfly. Besides hearing the angels sing, she was happily singing with the glorious choir and occasionally dancing like a graceful ballerina.

My friend Nancy Shankle commented how wonderful those words were. She said I should write. I shared with Nancy that I had always had a passion to write. I had made many attempts to pursue my dream but someone always crushed the desire. I had even taken a writing course thirty years ago, and after only two classes, my first husband beat me up and definitely extinguished any fire of enthusiasm I had had.

The next day as I was pulling out of the parking lot, Nancy pulled in and jumped out of her van and ran over to me. She reached in and grabbed my hands and began to pray over me. She prayed that God would remove whatever demons were blocking my writing. She continued to pray a blessing over me and walked away and left in her van. Wow! What just happened? That was amazing. I started to drive away feeling really strange. What a wonderful friend to care enough about me to take the time to pray over me.

About a week later, Nancy came into the workshop bubbling over with enthusiasm. She couldn't wait to tell me about a writer's group she had found out about. They were members of her church. She told them about me and they would love to have me join them. You can't even imagine how I felt. This was something I had always dreamed about, someone to show me the way. Someone who shared my same passion and could encourage me and these were spiritual women. Excited about this group gave me the best day ever. I danced around the workplace while my clients laughed at me. I couldn't wait to call the number Nancy had given me. Marykay, the leader of the class, answered the phone. I told her who I was, and she said that if I wanted to come that night, the group was meeting there in an hour. I said I would see her soon after she gave me the directions to her house.

This was really awkward for me to go somewhere where I didn't know anyone, but I was so excited. I felt uneasy walking to the front door, but soon it opened and I was inside among these fabulous women. They made

me feel so comfortable and invited me to have a seat in the living room. There must have been about nine women. They introduced themselves and I explained that I knew Nancy from their church. I told them how I had always wanted to write. One of the ladies said, "Great, for soon you will be writing." Marykay gave us a phrase and we had fifteen minutes to write a story that came to our mind. It was a good exercise to get our thoughts flowing free. It was fun although I could tell these experienced girls were much more creative in their writing than me. But I knew after time and some practice I would get better.

I loved being there with these caring women. They made me feel good about myself. After a few more writing prompts, Marykay started talking about the writer's retreat next month. My mouth fell open and my jaw dropped. I had heard about authors going away for a quiet time of writing, but never did I think that I would get a chance. Then I heard it was during the week. There goes my opportunity since I had to work. But wait, I knew I had some vacation time but didn't know how much. I told the group that I would love to go but needed to check with my husband. Then I would have to see if I could get the time off from work.

That evening when I got home, I was babbling to Bill about the upcoming writer's retreat and how much fun I had with the group. Bill was very encouraging but said I should see if I could get the time off from work. I figured I needed thirty-two hours.

The next morning I said a prayer then I called into the office at work. Guess what? I had exactly thirty-two

hours. I could not believe this. God was so amazing. I filled out the paperwork and put in for that time off quickly before someone snatched those days.

We met at the church parking lot with all of our stuff and baggage. We loaded up the cars and headed to the retreat. There were eleven of us going including me. We stopped along the way down and had dinner. After we were done eating, we were on the road again. It took about two hours to get there.

Pulling into the driveway of the retreat center, we could see the lake and the wooded area. This place was a paradise. The pastor from their church came with us and I had learned he had two books published and was here to work on his third. He was the only man with all of us women. We were so excited about our time away from the rat race of life. No responsibilities except to focus on our writing. Most of us were still in the stages of wondering where to begin, but there were some seasoned authors who were well under way with their books.

We carried our baggage into the retreat and were told where our rooms were. You can't even imagine the thrill and squealing when we found out that each room had its own bathroom and shower. Yes, we were in heaven for sure. This building used to be a seminary for priests. There were all kinds of places and cubby holes where each person could get away and write. There were libraries, a chapel, sunrooms, outside decks, benches by the lake, just to name a few. So many choices, each place could fit someone's personality where they could go and relax. You didn't always have to write. You could do what you wanted, just be respectful to the others who were

focused on their writing. We were going to be here for five days and four nights.

I loved my room. It had floral curtains that matched the tablecloth on the large round table. It was so peaceful and I really enjoyed the quiet time. I actually spent most of my time in there, but also loved the sunroom. Where do I begin? What was I going to write about? I had no idea. Maybe I should write the book with short inspirational stories. I had many stories I had written over the years. I kept them in a notebook. I also had a journal that was full of short stories. I always imagined I would write a book with inspirational short stories. But then again I felt that God wanted me to share my testimonial stories of Chris's recovery and the many rough times I had overcome. But that seemed so overwhelming and way too big of a project to start. We were given a folder with a book format to follow. It had questions to keep us on the purpose of why we wanted to write. Okay, let me start with a title for the book. I had no idea. This was going to be very interesting.

It was time for us all to gather and get to know each other. I was the new kid on the block. Most everyone else knew each other for years. They went to the same church or have been in the writing group. Marykay started out by explaining more about the outline and format of the structure of a book. We had our folders and we were following along. I enjoyed this since I knew I needed a lot of advice and instruction. Some of these people have published books and I was just so thrilled to be there among them. They included me in their conversations and I was making some new friends. After the meeting

we closed in prayer and we were free to do what we wanted. I headed back to my room. I was very tired.

After Tammy passed, so much had happened. Some of the staff had left their jobs and new people were hired. The structure of how I knew it changed drastically. The new managers came in with their ideas. I was struggling with the changes. I also know from experience that change isn't always bad. So I was determined to hang in there, especially since I loved working with my clients.

Tammy had been my artist and some of the other clients attempted to paint, but the painting wasn't the same. I had to fix most of their work. So getting away for this retreat was going to give me some time to think. This writer's retreat couldn't have come at a better time in my life. It was already mind boggling with what God was doing in my life. Bringing these wonderful spiritual friends who encouraged me to write was unbelievable. And here I was staying at this sacred place. Was this all for real? I really was beginning to think God was closing the door for me at the workshop. I was not happy there anymore.

In my room that night, it was so good just to have quiet time to think. Besides attempting to write, I was going to be praying about my work situation. Exhausted from preparing for this trip and my past few hectic days, I crawled into bed and fell fast asleep.

The next few days went fast. Some of the girls made great progress with their books. Others like me were just stumbling around with our ideas. I was thinking of using "Wind Beneath My Wings" as my title. I felt the short stories evolved around my broken wings from my

hardships in life. With God healing and mending my winds, I could fly free. I liked that idea until someone said you should not use song titles. That let the steam out of that idea, but I didn't care. I had already drawn a butterfly with a broken wing for my cover. I would use that title until I could come up with a better one.

After supper, we met in our gathering room to watch a movie. We were told it was about an author and his writing experiences and how he helped a young writer find his style. We passed out bowls of popcorn as we settled in our comfy chairs. The movie was great and the story line kept our attention.

We all enjoyed the movie and laughed at the funny parts. I was happy to share social time with my new friends. I got to learn more about their families and their lives as well as shared about myself. This was our last night at the retreat. I found a new family of soul sisters and my soul brother, Pastor Chuck.

The last day we worked on the back matter of the books. We had formed into two groups and went in different areas to work. Marykay was in my group and she, along with Cindy, both experienced writers, kept us on track. We spent time going over with each person's ideas for their book. Everyone would brainstorm and throw out ideas. We wrote down all the scribbles and notes until we finally agreed on the back matters of everyone's books. I was very impressed what we came up with for mine. It sounded so professional. After we had lunch, we tearfully loaded our suitcases and were ready for our long drive home. Our serenity and paradise was ending as we would soon be back in the reality of our

busy lives. We hugged and said good-bye and wished everyone good luck with their writing.

I awoke the next morning and headed off to work. I was glad it was Friday but sure could have used another day at the retreat. What was I going to do? As I clocked in I could feel the same stress that I didn't belong there. I was glad to see my clients and they were excited to hear about my book, and they told me I couldn't leave again. I smiled because they had no idea what I was thinking. So many of the original staff had left and I was the only one left at this workshop. I would keep doing my job until I felt sure that God was leading me elsewhere. I still had no passion or desire to paint for myself. And I wasn't actually positive I could write. Oh, I wanted to write, but would anyone want to read my stories?

My writing friends had invited me to attend their church on Sunday. I really enjoyed listening to Pastor Chuck talk about the retreat and admired everything about Marykay. Pastor Marykay was the associate pastor of the church. Nancy goes there and I had heard of the wonderful stories from my new friends.

I decided to go and I walked into the church Sunday and found a seat. Bill didn't want to go. This was a non-denomination church and we are Catholic. I have to admit it was a little more singing and praising God than I was used to. I did enjoy the message and also seeing some of my writing friends. Nancy was extremely happy to see me there. The people I didn't know reached out to welcome me. I could tell these people were all very loving Christians who were there for God. I left after church happy that I came.

I hadn't done any writing after I left the retreat. I was busy thinking about my job and whether I should leave. I used to love coming to work. Now I dreaded it. Bill could see how frustrated and depressed I was becoming. It depleted all my energy. I had put so much extra time in developing the painting area, and after Tammy died, it fell apart.

Pastor Marykay is a life purpose coach besides being an author and pastor. I decided to schedule some time to talk with her. I went after work the next week and she started by having me take a test that determines your personality type and which jobs best suit your personality. Wow, my test scores were right on. The structure of the workshop was completely incompatible to my personality. I need order and to be organized. Marykay agreed that my energy was being wasted from all this frustration.

I turned in my two-week notice. I was overcome with peace when I gave them that piece of paper. I knew from that moment I made the decision to leave that it was God's plan. The following week I celebrated my sixtieth birthday and qualified for my pension.

The first week of retirement I freshened up my studio, clearing a space to write. I let go of some clutter that had accumulated over the past year and a half of not painting. I packed up several boxes that had been stuff dragging around and I dropped them off at a donation center. That alone made the studio peaceful for a new beginning. As I was putting away some painting supplies, I looked tearfully at my watercolor pad. I had even tried to ignite the fire by taking some painting

classes last year. I struggled through those classes and still had no desire to paint.

I was curious to try it again. I loved being in my studio and I missed my painting—it was such a huge part of me. I brought out my brushes and set up my painting table ready to start. I decided to paint some red geraniums in a clay pot. Amazingly the colors of paint started flowing into a pretty picture. I kept painting and I started enjoying it again. I was delighted. My passion was back! Praising God, I had tears of joy released from deep inside. I cried and cried. I could not wait to show Bill the painting when he got home. He was so proud when he saw the picture and also thrilled to see the studio looking so nice again.

I continued painting every day. I had a nice assortment of artwork completed. God was doing something so awesome in my life. I could feel it. Every day something would happen, which confirmed God was there. My life was going so smoothly. I meditated and prayed every morning, I did my daily writing prompts, and after straightening up my home, I went to the studio. I felt so much peace. My attitude had changed. I was really calm about issues that I would have exploded in temper over before. Bill was thrilled with this new wife. She smiled again, and you could hear her humming while she painted. I organized our home. I had dinners prepared and the laundry was caught up and put away.

I started going to Bible study at the church with Pastor Marykay. I loved learning more about the word of God, especially with other women and their wisdom about the Bible. I purchased a new Bible and I was just

absorbing scripture like a sponge. I wanted to learn more, and I wanted to know Jesus.

At writing group last month, I was still struggling with a title for my book. I asked a few girls for suggestions and nothing touched my heart. All the other girls were making so much progress writing their books. Some were about to sign contracts with their publishers. I was praying and listening for God, and evidently he wasn't ready to give me an answer. Bill and I had been going to mass on Saturdays and I would go to High Mill Church on Sundays.

This Sunday after we had met at the writing group, God spoke loud and clear. As I was preparing to go to church, I heard him say, "Still dragging your stuff around?" I liked the way it sounded. It would be a perfect title for my book. At church during the praise and worship, they were singing about dragging your baggage around. Then Pastor Noah, Pastor Chuck's son, gave the sermon. My heart overflowed with excitement when he spoke about dragging your stuff around. Talk about confirmation. God was speaking loud and very clear. I had my title.

The next few weeks I had so much fire inside. I seriously could not stop writing. I wrote and I wrote day in and day out. The book was half written when the group scheduled another two-day retreat down to our sacred retreat center. Five of us were going down.

We arrived and found our rooms and retreated to our cubby holes of choice. Other than meals and a night of rest, we wrote and wrote. I was burning with desire to get these words out onto paper. God's words just flowed

through me. I was still writing up to the last eight minutes before we loaded the car and were heading back. I had written nine chapters in those two days. I, along with my loving soul family, was so impressed with all that I was able to write. I was finishing up my last few chapters.

After I got up the next morning, I started writing and God's words continued to flow through me and I finished the book. Yes, once I had the title, it took me three and a half weeks to write twenty-one chapters. I finally had the words out of my head and onto the paper—such a peaceful relief.

My life has become so wonderful, so peaceful. I pray for God's guidance every morning and praise him for all my blessings. I take time to read scripture and I listen for his whispers. I am not in a hurry to get everything done anymore. I just go with the flow, God's flow. I used to do everything my own way, stubborn, and I had to prove I was strong. I swam up stream many times never getting anywhere, and if I did, I usually was drowning in a big mess. I would have to dig my way out. I felt so free. Life went so easy, and my life is so content. Oh yes, life is life and things will go wrong, but I have a different outlook. I can actually feel God working through me with all the amazing things that have happened. He created me for his purpose and he has a plan much more glorious than I could ever imagine.

It has been nearly a year since my last session with my therapist, Amy. The last time we had talked about how far I had come and decided there was no reason for me to come back. I know I can always come back if I

feel I need to. I am so excited to make a trip to her office when this book is published so that I can happily and gratefully give her a signed copy.

I will forever be thankful for God using Nancy to bring me to High Mill Church. God knew how lonely I was and he brought me some spiritual, creative friends. These women have already learned how awesome our Savior is and saw life through Christ's eyes. The light of God shines through these people and I am so blessed to be among them.

Once I stopped dragging my stuff around and allowed God to take it from me, piece by piece, prayer by prayer he allowed me to find the forgiveness I desperately needed. I thought I had known God for years, but realize I had only slightly met him. There was so much more I needed to learn. Every day God brings new opportunities to learn and challenges to overcome. Life is not always easy. God never promised us that it would be easy. He promised if he brought you to it, he would bring you through it. Jesus loves us and he will never leave us. I realize that I am human and there will be times that I will be challenged with life and its circumstances. When those times come, I learned to spend time with Jesus and give the stuff to him. I will never bury the pain deep inside just to drag it around. I am learning the Bible and God gave us the answers inside this glorious book. Please don't keep dragging all your stuff around. Life is so much easier without all that baggage.

About the Author

SallyAnne Trissel is an author and artist who has a love for creativity. She believes in doing everything with a smile. SallyAnne and her husband, Bill, live in Canton, Ohio, with their four Cavalier King Charles Spaniels.